Clinical Research
Coordinator Handbook

Clinical Research
Coordinator Handbook
Third Edition

Deborrah Norris

Plexus Publishing, Inc.
Medford, New Jersey

First Printing, 2004

Clinical Research Coordinator Handbook, Third Edition

Library of Congress Cataloging-in-Publication Data

Norris, Deborrah.
  Clinical research coordinator handbook / Deborrah Norris.-- 3rd ed.
     p. ; cm.
  Includes bibliographical references.
  ISBN 0-937548-54-5 (pbk. : alk. paper)
  1. Clinical trials--United States--Handbooks, manuals, etc.
  [DNLM: 1. Clinical Trials--standards--United States--Handbooks. 2.
Clinical Trials--methods--United States--Handbooks. 3.
Records--standards--United States--Handbooks. 4. Research
Design--standards--United States--Handbooks. QV 39 N854c 2003] I.
Title.
  R853.C55N67 2004
  610'.7'2--dc22

                                                          2003020146

Publisher: Thomas H. Hogan, Sr.
Editor-in-Chief: John B. Bryans
Managing Editor: Deborah Poulson
Graphics Department Director: M. Heide Dengler
Illustrations: David Wetzel, Susan Gray, Bob Jackson,
            and David Beverage Graphic Design
Sales Manager: Pat Palatucci

Dedication

The third edition of this handbook is dedicated to clinical research professionals, worldwide.

To Francis X. Sexton, Jr. for his ethics, dedication, and commitment to always doing the right thing regardless of the consequences; and to Justin Norris—for continuing to make me proud to be your mother.

**In Memory of
Lawrence Ritchie, Jr., my brother,
and
Doris Sexton, my mother-in-law,
and
Edelyn Bleiweiss, former study subject and dear friend,
and
William Rodriguez, who was like a father to me**

Contents

Acknowledgments

It is with gratefulness and sincere appreciation that I acknowledge the assistance of many people in the third edition of this handbook. Throughout the revisions to this book, I have had a wonderful team cheering me on, offering advice, providing me with the push I needed to keep forging ahead, and having patience when the process took longer to complete.

Many, many thanks to those willing to share not only their wisdom and knowledge, but also taking time from their busy schedules to address my countless questions. To my superb editor, Deborah Poulson, for her unflagging enthusiasm, and to John Bryans and the wonderful people at Plexus Publishing, including Pat Palatucci, for keeping me on top of things.

To everyone who reviewed this edition of the handbook for their comments and suggestions, especially J. D. Davidson, Scott O'Neill, Lee Schwartzberg, M.D., James Matheney, and Kathleen Ventimiglia.

Geoff Green, working with you continues to be challenging and rewarding. J. D. Davidson, you knew me when … I am grateful not only for your taking time to write the foreword to this edition, but for your continued friendship these 20 years. Dr. Kevin Cleveland, Dr. Mario Werbin, and Joshlyn Potter, it is comforting to know, firsthand, that there are medical personnel willing to go the extra mile to ensure the best medical care possible. Thank you from the bottom of my heart. Viv, my pal, thank you for supporting me through those sad, dark days after my brother's death, and keeping me focused. Father James A. Quinn, thank you for always being there—St. Matthew will always have a special place in my heart. Once again, for technical expertise about the legal portions of this handbook, I went to my ultimate informed source, Francis X. Sexton, Jr., Esq. Any errors or oversights are mine. David Wetzel, Bob Jackson, and Susan Gray, your talent and illustrations continue to bring the chapters to life, while adding some humor. Moreover, as I have for many years, I relied on the wisdom and judgment of my foremost sounding boards, Justin and Frank. Thank you both for your support and love.

While things are changing drastically in the pharmaceutical industry, the Clinical Research Coordinator's role has become even more pivotal to the success of any clinical trial. **To all clinical research coordinators, you will always be the heart of research! I hope that the information in this handbook will continue to assist you in your clinical trials.**

Foreword

In this short book, you will find a straightforward explanation of clinical research and the role of the coordinator in such research. You will learn that, by following the details, paying attention to them, and maintaining an attitude of strict integrity, you can accomplish a creditable clinical research project.

Deborrah Norris has been doing clinical research longer than she will want me to admit. I have known her from her days as a college student, where she further honed her writing skills as a composition student of mine. She has always been a diligent worker who manages details very well. A strong work ethic and innate sense of integrity have been hallmarks of her work. A candid way of getting to the root of issues is manifested in this handbook. The humor throughout furnishes a welcome segue to the presentation.

Welcome to the world of clinical research!

J. D. Davidson
Dean of the Wasatch Campus
Utah Valley State College
Heber City, UT

I. Introduction

The purpose of this handbook is to outline the various functions required of the clinical research coordinator (CRC), research nurse, research assistant, data coordinator, or medical assistant involved in the conduct of a clinical study for an investigator on behalf of a pharmaceutical company or device manufacturer and Contract Research Organization (CRO)/Site Management Organization (SMO) (the Sponsor or Specialty Research Network).

The complete and accurate accumulation of information specified in the study protocol and the subsequent accurate transfer of this information to the case report form (CRF) is vital to the successful progress of a clinical study. As coordinators of this operation, CRCs play an integral role, often without the recognition and credibility they deserve for their dedication to this process. This handbook describes the various duties of CRCs and those assisting in the conduct of a clinical study. It outlines the regulatory requirements that MUST be followed when conducting a clinical study. The documentation that is required before the conduct of a study is described, and prototypes of forms, checklists, and letters are included. In addition, the topic of legal liability as it relates directly to the CRC has also been incorporated. A glossary of terms is located at the back of this handbook to aid in the understanding of the language of clinical research. Information regarding HIPAA regulations are also included.

Ultimately, it is the close communication between the investigator, CRC, and the sponsor that will ensure the timely and successful completion of the clinical study. Studies performed in accordance with their approved protocol, with the guidance of the sponsor, and under the supervision of a well-informed clinical research associate (CRA), will meet the goals of Good Clinical Practices (GCP) and the ICH guidelines, as well as the Federal Regulations as established by the Food and Drug Administration (FDA).

This handbook is written both as an introduction for the CRC who has not been involved in extensive clinical trials and as a refresher for the experienced CRC. In all cases, we are confident that the reader will gain a more detailed appreciation of the clinical study process.

II. Federal Regulations Governing the Obligations of Clinical Investigators of Regulated Articles

A clinical study is an experiment that has been designed to prove a hypothesis: for example, that Drug A is as safe and effective as Drug B; that a drug's pharmacokinetics remain unchanged in subjects with renal insufficiency; or that concomitant administration of an antacid with the drug has no effect on its absorption or other kinetic parameters. As with any other scientific endeavor, the conduct of a clinical study demands that good scientific methods be adhered to in order to ensure the highest quality results. Over the past several decades, clinical researchers have developed standard methods that, when implemented in a clinical study, contribute to its smooth progress. These methods may include the use of recognized screening criteria for assessing subject eligibility, such as the use of the DSM-IV to categorize mental illnesses or the use of American Rheumatology Association (ARA) criteria for determining the extent of involvement in subjects with rheumatoid arthritis. Other elements that add to the strength of the study include adherence to a well-defined clinical protocol, the selection of appropriate tests to assess safety and efficacy, the use of well-designed CRFs to ensure unbiased data collection, and the use of appropriately applied statistical tests for the analysis of the data.

Collectively, these elements form the basis for the concept of Good Clinical Practices (GCPs) and ICH guidelines. GCPs have been promulgated by the FDA with input from researchers, statisticians, clinical personnel, regulatory and legal specialists, and the pharmaceutical industry. They provide guidelines for essentially all aspects of conducting a well-designed and well-controlled clinical study. While it is the sponsor's responsibility to ensure that a study conforms to the guidelines set forth, the CRC and investigator must also assist the sponsor in adhering to these guidelines.

The regulations and guidelines of ICH and GCP are detailed, and the reader should recognize that the elements described in this manual are rooted in these concepts. The Code of Federal Regulations (CFR) 21CFR Part 50, "Protection of Human Subjects," and 21CFR312.50, Subpart D, "Responsibilities of Sponsors and Investigators," describe in detail the regulations set forth by the FDA regarding the testing of drugs in humans. Further FDA-related helpful sources can be found in Appendix I, Part B.

III. The Clinical Research Organization

A large portion of clinical studies sponsored by the pharmaceutical industry are implemented and monitored through contractual agreements with specialized providers of clinical services collectively known as CROs/SMOs or Specialty Networks.

A. Contract Research Organizations and Site Management Organizations

What They Are and What They Do

In the past, pharmaceutical companies supervised their own clinical trials, from the discovery of the compound, to animal testing, to the preliminary testing of human subjects, to the larger clinical trials involving hundreds or thousands of patients. To assist pharmaceutical companies, CROs/SMOs/Specialty Networks have developed to handle all of that and more.

Contract research organizations are composed of companies that run parts or all of the clinical trials. Site management organizations generally are a group of physicians willing to offer their services to conduct the actual clinical trials. Specialty Networks are composed of sites in a specific medical Specialty that not only perform clinical trials but also offer additional services assisting in the conduct of clinical trials. These organizations arose to fill a need, to assist the pharmaceutical companies in the drug development process. According to an article in the *New York Times* published in May 1999, these organizations evolved to elevate the enormous pressure that began around 1992 from managed care companies and health insurers on drug companies to hold down prices. The FDA encouraged development of these companies in order to speed up its approval process. The average review time for new drug applications (NDAs) dropped from more than 22 months in 1990 to just over 14 months in 1997, according to the FDA.

Pharmaceutical companies found they had to invest more effort and revenue into finding drugs to develop, while at the same time cutting their development costs. For many pharmaceutical companies, the solution was to dismantle all or part of their clinical research monitoring departments that ran the clinical trials, turning the work over to smaller companies that had emerged to fill the industry's needs.

Contract research organizations can assist the pharmaceutical companies by:

- ✔ designing the protocol, CRFs, and source documents required for each clinical trial;

- ✔ locating principal investigators (PIs);

- ✔ assisting in potential patient recruitment efforts;

- ✔ statistically analyzing the clinical trial data;

- ✔ meeting with the FDA;

- ✔ preparing the enormous amount of paperwork required by the FDA for submission before the test article can be approved;

- ✔ writing the scientific papers for publication and presentation at national and international scientific meetings;

- ✔ conducting periodic auditing of investigator sites to ensure the study is being conducted according to the protocol, the CODE OF FEDERAL REGULATIONS, and GCP;

- ✔ selecting and coordinating central laboratories; and

- ✔ selecting and coordinating independent institutional review boards (IRBs).

Site management organizations and specialty networks can assist the pharmaceutical industry by:

- ✔ providing a national network of physicians experienced in a specific therapeutic area (such as oncology, cardiology, and neurology) in conducting clinical trials;

- ✔ coordinating the completion of the required regulatory documents for their sites;

- ✔ providing technology to assist in the conduct of a clinical study;

- ✔ negotiating the budget for their sites;

- ✔ handling the financial aspects of the clinical trial for their sites, invoicing the sponsor, and providing payment to their sites;

- ✔ providing ongoing training to their sites;

- ✔ providing tools for their sites to meet enrollment commitments;

- ✔ providing their sites with a set of standard operating procedures (SOPs);

- ✔ developing study-specific source documents for their sites; and

- ✔ providing data coordinators to assist in the completion of the case report forms (CRFs).

In addition to providing these services, several organizations have a Phase I unit, on-site or off-site, where they can conduct clinical trials introducing the test article for the first time to healthy human subjects.

The size of these organizations varies from large corporations, to groups of physicians conducting clinical trials in a specialized area such as oncology and urology, to a rolodex of the names of physicians interested in participating in clinical trials, to a directory of physicians by specialty, to a Web site listing clinical trials seeking PIs, to a company of one person working out of her/his home to develop a drug.

Due to the nature of clinical research, these organizations will continue to provide the pharmaceutical industry with the necessary support needed to conduct clinical trials. The CRC and PI play pivotal roles in ensuring the smooth conduct of a study. By understanding all elements of the clinical protocol, the CRFs, and the study design, the CRC, PI, CRO/SMO/Specialty Networks, and Sponsor will be able to work together to efficiently meet the study goals.

B. Good Clinical Practice Guidelines

What Is Good Clinical Practice?

Good Clinical Practice or "GCP" is a standard for the:

- ✔ Design
- ✔ Conduct
- ✔ Performance
- ✔ Monitoring
- ✔ Auditing
- ✔ Recording
- ✔ Analyses
- ✔ Reporting

of clinical trials.

Good Clinical Practice (GCP) ensures the rights and safety of clinical trial subjects and the integrity of clinical data obtained during the conduct of a clinical trial. GCP concerns everyone working on *any* aspect of clinical research.

GCP guidelines were developed to ensure that only adequately planned and conducted clinical trials are performed in order to safeguard the interests of the patient, investigator, Sponsor, and the general community.

What Is the International Council of Harmonization?

The International Council of Harmonization (ICH) is an international standard for the:

✔ Design

✔ Conduct

✔ Performance

✔ Monitoring

✔ Auditing

✔ Recording

✔ Analyses

✔ Reporting

that provides assurance that the clinical data obtained and reported results during the conduct of a clinical trial are credible and accurate and that the rights, integrity, and confidentiality of study subjects are protected.

C. Declaration of Helsinki

The Declaration of Helsinki states:

✔ Research must conform to scientific principles.

✔ Protocols must be approved by an independent ethics committee.

✔ Clinical trials must be supervised and conducted by suitably qualified persons.

✔ Objectives and possible benefits must be balanced against the risk to the human subject.

✔ Privacy of the human subject must be respected and there is minimal physical and mental impact on the subject.

✔ Informed consent must be obtained from a potential human subject prior to the performance of *any* study-related procedures.

D. Sponsor of a Clinical Trial

The Sponsor of a clinical trial is an individual or organization responsible for the initiation, management, and/or financing of clinical trials. The Sponsor of a clinical trial is generally the organization that possesses permission from the appropriate regulatory agency to conduct the clinical trial. In most instances, the sponsor is a pharmaceutical company.

Sponsor responsibilities include:

- ✔ Providing the Investigational study trial material
- ✔ Providing technology to assist in the conduct of a clinical study
- ✔ Providing a protocol and ensuring protocol compliance
- ✔ Providing monitoring and source data verification
- ✔ Maintaining study trial material disposition records
- ✔ Data Management
- ✔ Record retention of the study-related documents
- ✔ Providing compensation and indemnity for clinical trial related injury
- ✔ Assuring the quality of the clinical trial data

IV. Investigator Responsibilities

A. Condensed Version

Administrative

✔ Review Protocol, Investigator Brochure, Conventions

✔ Communication with Institutional Review Board

✔ Hospital Management (in-patient study)

✔ Curriculum vitae

✔ Informed Consent

✔ Records and Reports

✔ Delegation of tasks specific to the clinical trial

Logistics

✔ Sufficient time to conduct study/adequate staff/facilities

✔ Ensure all research staff adequately informed

✔ List of delegated study-related tasks and the names of those qualified to perform the tasks

Study Drug Management

✔ Full study drug accountability documentation

• Receipt of the investigational product

✔ Inventory, return, disposition of the investigational product

• Properly used by patients

✔ Safe and proper handling and storage of the investigational product

✔ Ensure patient compliance with the investigational product

✔ Randomization procedures conducted according to the protocol

✔ Unblinding procedures conducted according to the protocol

- Disclosure envelopes containing study drug/placebo information
- Emergency situation

Informed Consent

✔ Informed consent must be approved by an Institutional Review Board (IRB)

✔ Must be obtained prior to the performance of any study-related procedure and documented in the clinical records

✔ Consent obtained in writing

✔ Use of correct version of the informed consent

✔ Signed and personally dated by the patient or the patient's legal representative

✔ Provide copy of the fully executed informed consent to the patient

✔ Inform the patient if there is any new information that may impact the patient's continued participation in the study

INFORMED CONSENT IS A PROCESS—NOT JUST A WRITTEN DOCUMENT.

Safety Reporting

✔ Adverse events/laboratory abnormalities

✔ Expedited reporting

Data Collection

✔ Case report forms completed properly, completely, and in a timely manner

✔ Make data available for monitoring audit

✔ Indicate ongoing review of subjects labs and procedure reports by dating and initialing when reviewed

B. Clinical Trial Monitoring of Documentation

Purpose of Monitoring:

✔ To verify that informed consent was obtained prior to the conduct of any study-related procedures

✔ To verify the protocol is being conducted appropriately

✔ To verify the study subjects have met the inclusion and exclusion criteria and, if applicable, to verify a waiver was granted by the appropriate study personnel and a copy of the waiver signed by the person granting the waiver is on file

- ✔ To verify all primary and secondary efficacy variables

- ✔ To review all pertinent patient safety information, including serious adverse events, adverse events, study procedures being followed according to the protocol and to document if any protocol procedures are not being followed (e.g., study procedures not being performed), patients enrolled into the clinical trial without meeting the inclusion/exclusion criteria, and not obtaining a waiver from the appropriate study personnel

- ✔ To verify the study drug is being stored, dispensed, and returned correctly and that appropriate study drug accountability records are being maintained

- ✔ To verify that the information contained in the Case Report Forms (CRFs) is accurate and verifiable with source documentation

C. Investigator Responsibilities

When a Principal Investigator signs the form FDA 1572, he/she makes the following commitments:

1. Agrees to conduct the study(ies) in accordance with the relevant, current protocol(s) and will only make changes in a protocol *after* notifying the Sponsor, except when necessary to protect the safety, rights, or welfare of subjects.

2. Agrees to *personally* conduct or supervise the described investigation(s).

3. Agrees to inform any patient or any person used as controls that the drugs are being used for investigational purposes and will ensure that the requirements relating to obtaining informed consent in 21 CFR Part 50 and institutional review board (IRB) review and approval in 21 CFR Part 56 are met.

4. Agrees to report to the sponsor adverse experiences that occur in the course of the investigation(s) in accordance with 21 CFR Part 312.64.

5. Acknowledges understanding of the information in the Investigator Brochure, including the potential risks and side effects of the drug.

6. Agrees to ensure that all associates, colleagues, and employees assisting in the conduct of the study(ies) are informed about their obligations in meeting these stated commitments.

7. Agrees to maintain adequate and accurate records in accordance with 21 CFR 312.62 and to make those records available for inspection in accordance with 21 CFR 312.68.

8. Ensures that an IRB that complies with the requirements of 21 CRF Part 56 will be responsible for the initial and continuing review and approval of the clinical investigation.

9. Agrees to promptly report to the IRB all changes in the research activity and all unanticipated problems involving risks to human subjects.

10. Agrees to not make any changes in the research protocol without IRB approval, except when necessary to eliminate apparent immediate hazards to human subjects.

11. Agrees to comply with all other requirements regarding the obligations of clinical investigators and all other pertinent requirements in 21 CFR Part 312.

These commitments are considered essential to the success of a clinical trial in accordance with FDA regulations, Good Clinical Practice, and ICH guidelines.

Principal Investigator

The Principal Investigator (PI) of a clinical trial must be qualified by education, training in the therapeutic area of the clinical trial being conducted by the applicable regulatory requirements (Code of Federal Regulations, GCP and ICH Guidelines). The PI must be familiar with the investigational product being used in the clinical trial and must also comply with the applicable regulatory requirements.

The PI is ultimately responsible for the conduct of a clinical trial at a trial site as well as the integrity, health and welfare of the human subjects during the clinical trial.

Principal Investigator Responsibilities

The responsibilities of the PI include:

✔ Obtaining informed consent from a patient prior to the performance of *any* study-related procedures, including documentation in the patient's clinical chart that written informed consent was obtained prior to the performance of any study-related procedures

✔ Ensuring the Informed Consent Document was approved by an Institutional Review Board and the correct version of the informed consent is being used

✔ Complying with the Institutional Review Board (IRB) approved protocol

✔ Maintaining study trial material accountability

✔ Medically supervising the conduct of the clinical trial

✔ Maintaining adequate patient records and Case Report Forms (CRFs)

✔ Maintaining the site facilities and staff and ensuring both are adequate to perform the study-related procedures

✔ Enrolling the adequate number of study patients required by the Sponsor

✔ Ensuring adequate reporting of Adverse Events (AEs) and Serious Adverse Events (SAEs) according to the Federal Regulations

✔ Archiving study-related documents for the time period required by the Sponsor

Principal Investigator Responsibilities and Informed Consent

The PI, or a person designated by the PI, should fully inform the potential subject of all pertinent aspects of the clinical trial. Documentation is necessary to ensure study-related procedures were not performed prior to the signing of the informed consent document. The informed consent document must be signed, dated, and witnessed by an unbiased third party. While this is not always possible, it is preferred.

Who Should Administer Informed Consent?

ICH 4.8.5 states "The Investigator, or a person designated by the investigator, should fully inform the subject…"
ICH 2.1 states "Clinical trials should be conducted in accordance with the ethical principles that have their origin in the Declaration of Helsinki…"

Declaration of Helsinki B (21) states, "The physician should then obtain the subject's freely-given informed consent…"

The ultimate responsibly of administering informed consent still resides with the PI. An auditor would expect the required documentation, reassurance that the PI is knowledgeable, and that a physician was available at the time of consent, if applicable, to answer medically related questions. In addition, in the documentation in the potential clinical trial subject's chart, there must be proof that consent was obtained prior to performing any study-related procedures. It should note the time the informed consent was obtained, providing reassurance that informed consent was obtained correctly.

Adhering to the Approved Study Protocol

A Principal Investigator conducting clinical trials must adhere to the approved study protocol. The PI ensures that the protocol and amendments are strictly followed. The PI agrees not to make any changes to the study procedures without prior agreement of the Sponsor and the IRB, except when necessary to eliminate apparent immediate hazard to a study subject. The PI documents and explains any deviation from the approved protocol and the reason for the deviation. If a study procedure is not conducted according to the protocol, it is generally considered a protocol violation. If, prior to the study procedure deviation, permission is given from the Sponsor and/or Study Medical Monitor, it is frequently considered a waiver. For instance: Patient #0003 did not return to the clinic for protocol-specific procedures and did not notify the PI. If this was noted during a regular monitoring visit, it would be considered to be a protocol violation. However, if this same patient were to inform the PI he or she would not be able to return to the clinic on the specified day for protocol-specific procedures and the PI contacted the Sponsor and/or the Medical Monitor, a waiver could be granted. There can be no waiver or protocol exception for a deviation from the protocol *after* it has occurred. This is one reason communication between the PI, the PI's staff, the monitor, and the Sponsor is of critical importance.

Study Drug Accountability

The PI is ultimately responsible for maintaining study drug accountability. The PI and/or a pharmacist or other designated study personnel should maintain records of the product's delivery to the site. This includes the product's inventory at the site, the use by each subject and the return of the used/returned or unused products to the Sponsor or alternate disposition of the unused product(s). ***It is important to note: Returned/dispensed study products should not be kept in the same area, since the study drug is not yet dispensed.***

Study Drug Accountability Records are maintained to include the dates, quantities, batch/serial numbers, expiry dates, and unique code numbers. It is important to provide instructions for the correct use of the study drug. It is also important to remember that the Study Coordinator or the pharmacist may dispense study medication only under the supervision of the PI or subinvestigator listed on the FDA 1572.

If the study drug is transported from one satellite center to another, (if applicable) it is important to have a written policy and a procedure in place to document that the integrity of the study drug was maintained during the transporting. *Prior* approval must be obtained from the Sponsor before the study drug is transported from one center to another. Some centers have forms in place that document the date, time, and person transporting the study drug as well as document the date, time, and name of the person receiving the study drug. If the study drug requires refrigeration or room temperature, the measures taken to ensure the required temperature must be documented to protect the integrity of the study drug.

The study drug should only be dispensed to the person actually taking the medication. It is not acceptable for a wife or husband to pick up the study drug for a partner. It is also a good idea to make sure the study patient returns the unused study medication (including the package) before additional study drug is dispensed. In rare instances this may not be possible; however, it would be a good idea to contact the monitor or Sponsor prior to dispensing the medication in order to obtain a waiver if applicable.

Medical Supervision of the Clinical Trial

The Principal Investigator must be responsible for all study-related medical decisions; this includes the supervision of all adverse events, dose changes, and informing the study patient about intercurrent illnesses.

The PI must maintain adequate patient records, which should include the following:

- ✔ Patient demographics.
- ✔ Date of the study visit or unscheduled visit.
- ✔ Documentation that the patient consented to participate in the clinical trial and that no study-related procedures were performed prior to obtaining the informed consent. It is also a good idea to note the time consent was obtained.
- ✔ Patient eligibility and verification the patient has met the inclusion/exclusion criteria required by the protocol.

- ✔ Concomitant medications and the indications for the medication (it is a good idea to make sure the medication the patient is taking is consistent with the patient's medical history).

- ✔ Document all adverse events reported by the patient as required by the protocol.

- ✔ Appropriate HIPAA documentation.

Maintain Adequate Site Facilities and Staff

The Principal Investigator should have available an adequate number of qualified staff members and adequate facilities for the foreseeable duration of the clinical trial. This would include calibration of equipment used during the study and the retention of equipment service records. The PI also ensures all staff members assisting with the clinical trial are adequately trained and knowledgeable about the protocol, the procedures, and the investigational product(s) and their role and responsibilities in the clinical trial.

Maintain Adequate Number of Study Subjects

The Principal Investigator should be able to demonstrate a potential for recruiting the required number of study subjects eligible to participate in the clinical trial within the agreed recruitment period. In addition, the PI must have sufficient time to properly conduct and complete the clinical trial within the agreed clinical trial period.

Investigator Responsibilities

The Principal Investigator is responsible for reporting adverse events (AEs) and serious adverse events (SAEs) experienced by subjects participating in a clinical trial. The PI must immediately inform the Sponsor of any serious or unexpected adverse event occurring during the clinical trial. The PI must notify the IRB or Independent Ethics Committee (IEC) of these events. All serious adverse events are accompanied by an assessment of causality and possible impact on the clinical trial. It is not appropriate to delegate this responsibility to the Study Coordinator or the Research Nurse, regardless of their experience. This is a function that must be performed by the PI or the subinvestigator.

Archiving Study Documents

The Principal Investigator must retain records and data from the clinical trial for safety reasons and for audit and inspection subsequent to study completion. The records must be maintained in a secure area in order to prevent undue access, loss, or tampering. Unless specified in the protocol, the study records must be maintained for no less than 15 years. In some cases the issue of product liability may dictate longer retention time by Sponsors.

As a Principal Investigator, it is important to remember that you can delegate a task—but never the responsibility.

V. Duties of the Clinical Research Coordinator

The CRC or Research Nurse plays a pivotal role in the efficient progress of the clinical study. The CRC is often responsible for organizing the documentation and files pertaining to a study and for coordinating the subsequent activities of the investigators and subjects. The responsibilities of the CRC will vary at each investigational site, but may include the following:

✔ to review and familiarize themselves and other staff with the protocol;

✔ to provide prospective investigators with a copy of the protocol;

✔ to notify the Sponsor and CRO/SMO/Specialty Network of investigators' interest in participating in the study;

✔ to prepare a grant (if needed) in conjunction with the sponsor;

✔ to compile the required information for the Sponsor and CRO/SMO/Specialty Network;

✔ to review FDA requirements and ICH and GCP guidelines;

✔ to prepare for the IRB meeting, including preparation of the Informed Consent document (to be forwarded to the sponsor before the IRB meeting) and other prestudy documentation, preparation of the meeting agenda, and mailing of the IRB meeting notice to investigators;

✔ to attend the IRB meeting and to have proposed IRB approval letters ready (both the PI and the CRC should attend, if possible);

✔ to identify the study site's contact person;

✔ to establish the need for a Letter of Indemnification from the Sponsor;

✔ to schedule on-site visits with the Sponsor;

✔ to participate in the investigator meeting;

- ✔ to prepare additional study records, forms, and letters as directed by the CRO/SMO/Specialty Network or Sponsor;

- ✔ to set up study files;

- ✔ to enroll subjects;

- ✔ to oversee study activities, including the secure storage of the test article;

- ✔ to maintain accurate and complete records; and

- ✔ to close the study with the sponsor and to store the study records appropriately.

A. Compiling Prestudy Documents

Before subjects can be enrolled in a study and before test articles can be shipped, several prestudy documents must be compiled by the CRC or investigator and sent for approval to the Sponsor. Descriptions of these documents follow.

Form FDA 1572. This is the Statement of Investigator form, which summarizes what the FDA requires for an acceptable clinical study. It must be signed by the PI. In addition, all subinvestigators (if any) who are participating in the study and who are authorized to administer the test articles must be listed. In most instances, the Sponsor determines which study personnel is required on the Form FDA 1572. The actual form, along with a sample of a completed version, is provided in Appendix II (Form 2). Investigators who sign Form FDA 1572 make the following commitments:

- ✔ to conduct the study according to the protocol (Changes made to the protocol can be made after notification to the sponsoring pharmaceutical company, except to protect patient safety. Investigators who deviate from the protocol for any reason need also to notify their IRB in writing of the deviation);

- ✔ to personally conduct and/or supervise the research protocol;

- ✔ to inform patients that they are participating in a research study;

- ✔ to abide by the IRB and Informed Consent regulations;

- ✔ to report all serious adverse events according to Federal Regulations to the sponsoring pharmaceutical company and the IRB;

- ✔ to read and understand the *Investigator Brochure* for the investigational material being tested;

- ✔ to ensure that other personnel involved with the study meet these commitments;

- ✔ to maintain accurate study records and to make these records available for inspection by the appropriate agencies (FDA and the sponsoring pharmaceutical company and their representatives);

✔ to ensure initial and continuing review and approval of the research study by the IRB; and

✔ to comply with the Federal Regulations for investigators in 21 CFR 312.

Note: the PI may delegate some of these responsibilities to the CRC, but, ultimately, the PI is responsible for ensuring that they are done correctly.

Curricula Vitae (CV). These are required of the PI and all the subinvestigators listed on Form FDA 1572. Curricula vitae should be updated every two years, and they should be signed and dated to show that they are current. A copy of the physician's medical license as well as proof of malpractice insurance may be required by some sponsors. In addition, CVs of the CRC and the laboratory director, if appropriate (i.e., when a central laboratory is used by a Sponsor), may also be required.

Lab Certification. A copy of the laboratory license, laboratory certification, and the normal laboratory values for the laboratory to be used must be on file.

Signed Protocol. This must be signed and dated by the PI, along with any protocol amendments.

Financial Certification/Disclosure. The following are the necessary financial certification/ disclosure requirements:

✔ Every PI needs to certify/disclose if she/he has a financial interest in the sponsoring pharmaceutical company or in the investigational material being tested.

✔ Certification is required for each PI and all subinvestigators listed on Form FDA 1572.

✔ This certification encompasses not only the investigator, but also her/his spouse and each dependent child.

✔ The certification is applicable for the time during which the PI is conducting the study and for one year following completion of the study (i.e., after enrollment of all subjects and follow-up subjects, in accordance with the protocol). The sponsoring pharmaceutical company should be notified in writing of any change in the accuracy of the certification during the clinical trial.

✔ Any financial interest in the sponsoring pharmaceutical company or in the product being tested needs to be promptly disclosed to the sponsoring pharmaceutical company.

Specifically, each PI must certify/disclose that she/he:

✔ has not entered into any financial arrangement with the sponsoring pharmaceutical company, whereby the outcome of the clinical study could affect her/his compensation (e.g., bonus, royalty, or other financial incentive);

✔ does not have a proprietary interest in the study material (e.g., patent, trademark, copyright, licensing agreement, etc.);

✔ does not have a significant equity interest in the sponsoring pharmaceutical company, not applicable to the material being tested; and

✔ has not received significant payments or money or anything of value from the sponsoring pharmaceutical company with a value in excess of $25,000, other than payments for conducting the clinical study (e.g., grants, compensation in the form of equipment, retainers for ongoing consultation and honoraria paid to the investigator or to the institution in support of the PI's activities).

Other documents that are required to be on file before a study may begin include the IRB approval and membership list, the budget for the study, the Letter of Agreement between the Sponsor and CRO/SMO or investigator, and the approved Informed Consent Form. The sponsor will inform the CRC of the documents needed at each step of the study. The Administrative Checklist (see Appendix II, Form 3) provides a mechanism to determine if appropriate documentation has been obtained and completed.

B. Creating and Maintaining Study Files

The Study File. Once all prestudy documents have been compiled, the Study File should be created. This file will be maintained throughout the clinical study and will eventually contain samples of all forms and reports to be completed during the course of the study, in addition to all prestudy documents.

Initially, the following materials should be included in the Study File:

✔ Prestudy documents, including:

   ✔ Form FDA 1572;

   ✔ current, signed, and dated (within two years) Curricula Vitae of investigators, CRC, and laboratory director;

   ✔ current medical license;

   ✔ proof of malpractice insurance (if required);

   ✔ Financial Disclosure Form;

   ✔ Investigational New Drug (IND) Application, safety letters, if applicable;

   ✔ current laboratory certification and normal ranges for laboratory values;

- ✔ Protocol (including Signature Page and Synopsis), including amendments to the protocol;

- ✔ current IRB membership list;

- ✔ IRB approval;

- ✔ IRB-approved Informed Consent Form;

- ✔ IRB-approved advertising, including any written information provided to a subject during the study;

- ✔ Investigator Brochure (all versions);

- ✔ Test Article Inventory and Drug Accountability Record;

- ✔ Completed and signed Delegation of Responsibilities Form;

- ✔ CRFs and Adverse Experience Forms;

- ✔ Completed and signed Authorized Representative Signature Record;

- ✔ Specimen Submission Records (if required);

- ✔ Site Visit Log;

- ✔ Telephone Log;

- ✔ IRB Fee Letter;

- ✔ Letter of Indemnification; and

- ✔ all correspondence to and from Sponsor.

The CRA will review the Study File with the CRC at the beginning of the study to ensure that all of the required documentation is present.

As the study progresses, additional documents will be completed. These (or copies) should be retained in the Study File. Examples include:

- ✔ amendments to the Protocol;

- ✔ executed Informed Consent Forms;

- ✔ laboratory test results;

- ✔ shipping invoices for all test articles, Returned Goods Form/destruction forms, if applicable;

- ✔ ongoing correspondence;

- ✔ other source documents;

✔ miscellaneous Sponsor forms;

✔ revised Informed Consent Forms; and

✔ correspondence to and from the IRB regarding the progress of the study, Protocol deviations, and submission of IND Safety Reports.

If a copy of a form is kept in another file, the original should be readily available and its location should be noted in a memo to the Investigator File.

The Subject Workfolder. Subject Workfolders must also be compiled for each subject enrolled in the study. When correctly organized, these greatly facilitate the proper collection of study data and form the core of the clinical database. Each Workfolder should contain the following, as appropriate:

✔ Study Design Flow Chart;

✔ Screening Sheet (Inclusion/Exclusion Criteria);

✔ Informed Consent Form (two signed copies—one for the research chart and one for the subject);

✔ Laboratory Requisitions Packet;

✔ Data Collection Form from CRF;

✔ specimen labels;

✔ chest radiographs (if required);

✔ disbursement requests (compensation vouchers);

✔ a "Stop!—Research Subject" sign (see Appendix II, Forms 14 and 15);

✔ clinic statements;

✔ synopsis of Protocol;

✔ letters to the subject;

✔ worksheet for outside departments; and

✔ Medical Release of Information for medical records.

Each document in the Subject Workfolder should be identified with a unique subject number. For example, 103A-207 may indicate Protocol 103A, site number 2, patient number 7.

The Audit File. At the conclusion of a study, an Audit File will be created. This will contain portions of the Study File, including:

✔ Site Visit Log;

✔ Telephone Log;

✔ Protocol (all versions, including amendments);

✔ Informed Consent Form (all versions used during the study);

✔ Drug Receipt/Return Log/destruction form, if applicable;

✔ Subject Drug Dispensation Log;

✔ prestudy documents;

✔ correspondence; and

✔ Financial Disclosure (See Appendix II, Form 12).

C. Obtaining CLIA Laboratory Certification as It Pertains to Clinical Research

CLIA. The Clinical Lab Improvement Amendment of 1988 (CLIA) is a federal program established by Congress to improve the quality and reliability of clinical labs. CLIA requires that all clinical labs be certified through the Health Care Financing Administration (HCFA). HCFA is a division of the U.S. Department of Health and Human Services (DHHS). The Department of Health in each state administers the CLIA program for their own state; however, lab certificates are issued through HCFA and are signed by an authorized HCFA representative. You will see a CLIA certificate sample later in the module.

Types of CLIA Certificates

The following are different types of CLIA certificates and can be issued to a lab upon inspection, depending on the types of testing it performs:

✔ Laboratory Certificate of Registration

✔ Laboratory Certificate of Compliance

✔ Laboratory Certificate of Accreditation

✔ Laboratory Certificate of Provider-Performed Microscopy Procedures (PPMP)

✔ Laboratory Certificate of Waiver

The following chart lists the three types of test classifications (types of test performed by a lab) and acceptable certificates for each classification. You must be familiar with the types of tests and acceptable certificates in order to verify that each lab has appropriate CLIA documentation while conducting a clinical trial.

Acceptable CLIA Certificates	
Test Classification	**Certificate(s) Required**
Moderate-to-Highly Complex Tests	CLIA Laboratory Certificate of Compliance **OR** Private Agency Certificate of Accreditation and a CLIA Laboratory Certficate of Accreditation • Whether a test is moderate or highly complex is dependent on the number of manual steps involved in completing the test and the level of interpretation required. For example, highly complex tests involve several critical steps and a high level of interpretation.

	Examples of moderately complex tests include:
	   – Liver enzymes
	   – Electrolytes
	   – PT / PTT
	
	Examples of highly complex tests include:
	   – HIV testing
	   – Manual cell counts
	   – DNA PCR tests
	   – Electrophoresis

Microscopy Procedures	CLIA Laboratory Certificate of Provider-Performed Microscopy Procedures • Microscopies include substances that a physician views under the microscope. For example, vaginal smears and semen.
Waived Tests	CLIA Laboratory Certificate of Waiver • Waived tests are laboratory examinations and procedures that have been approved by the FDA for home use or have been determined to be simple laboratory examinations and procedures that have an insignificant risk of an erroneous result.

Example of waived tests include:

- Dipstick or tablet reagent urinalysis (nonautomated) for bilirubin, glucose, ketones, hemoglobin, specific gravity, leukocytes, nitrates, protein, pH, and urobilinogen
- Fecal occult blood
- Ovulation test—visual color comparison test for human luteinizing hormone
- Urine prenancy test—visual color comparison tests
- Erythrocyte sedimentation rate (nonautomated)
- Blood glucose by blood glucose monitoring devices cleared by the FDA specifically for home use
- Spun microhematocrit

CLIA Certificate Descriptions

Now that you are familiar with the types of CLIA certificates, let us take a closer look at each one.

CLIA Certificate	Description
Laboratory Certificate of Registration	• Every lab that applies for a Certificate of Compliance or a Certificate of Accreditation receives this certificate. • Each lab is assigned a CLIA ID#—this number appears on all CLIA certificates. • This certificate indicates that the lab is registered with the HCFA through the State Department of Health—it **does not** indicate that the lab is in compliance with federal CLIA requirements. • Laboratories applying for a Certificate of Compliance or a Certificate of Accreditation operate under the Certificate of Registration until the State Department of Health completes an inspection of the lab.

	• If the inspection is not conducted within 1 year, HCFA will renew the certificate for 1 more year, until the inspection is performed.
Laboratory Certificate of Compliance	• This certificate is issued to labs conducting moderate-to-highly complex testing. • The certificate is issued by HCFA after the State Department of Health has inspected the lab. • Labs operate under the Certificate of Registration until they receive the Certificate of Compliance. • Labs with this certificate can also perform microscopy procedures and waived tests. • The Certificate of Compliance is a stand-alone document.
Laboratory Certificate of Accreditation	• This certificate is issued to labs conducting moderate-to-highly complex testing. • After the lab contacts an approved Private Accrediting Agency the agency conducts an inspection. If the lab passes inspection, the Private Accrediting Agency will issue its Certificate of Accreditation. • The Private Accrediting Agency notifies HCFA that the lab passed inspection. • HCFA then issues a CLIA Laboratory Certificate of Accreditation based on inspection results. • Labs operate under the Certificate of Registration until they receive the Certificate of Accreditation. • Labs with this certificate can also perform microscopy procedures and waived tests. • The Certificate of Accreditation **is not** a stand-alone document. The CLIA Certificate of Accreditation must be accompanied by the Certificate of Accreditation issued by the Private Accrediting Agency.
Certificate of Provider-Performed Microscopy Procedures	• This certificate is issued to labs that perform microscopy procedures. • The certificate **does not** require an inspection. However,

	labs can be subject to an inspection if a complaint about them is made to the State Department of Health.
	• Labs applying for a Certificate of Provider-Performed Microscopy Procedures **do not** receive a CLIA Certificate of Registration.
	• A lab with this certificate can also perform waived tests.
	• The Certificate of Provider-Performed Microscopy Procedures is a stand-alone document.
Certificate of Waiver	• This certificate is issued to labs that only perform waived tests.
	• Labs that only perform waived tests are waived from routine inspections, proficiency testing, quality assurance, quality control, and lab personnel requirements.
	• The certificate does not require an inspection. However, labs can be subject to an inspection if a complaint about them is made to the State Department of Health.
	• Labs applying for a Certificate of Waiver **do not** receive a CLIA Certificate of Registration.
	• The Certificate of Waiver is a stand-alone document.

It can take several months for HCFA to issue a CLIA Laboratory Certificate. If the certificate expires during the conduct of a clinical trial and the lab director has applied for a Certificate of Registration but has not yet received it:

✔ Ask the lab for their CLIA ID#.

✔ Ask the lab to provide you with a letter of notification from their State Department of Health. This letter should acknowledge that the lab has applied for CLIA certification and should include their CLIA ID#.

CLIA Certificate Sample

The following page shows a sample of a CLIA Laboratory Certificate of Accreditation. Note that the certificate has some important key elements. The certificate:

Department of Health & Human Services

Health Care Financing Administration

Laboratory:	Clinical Labs, Inc.	**CLIA ID#: 07D0092519**
Mailing Address:	4321 Stanton St. Cincinnati, OH 55155	**Effective Date:** October 2004
Laboratory Director:	John Ninane	**Expiration Date:** November 2006
Physical Location:	4321 Stanton St. Cincinnati, OH 55155	

CLIA LABORATORY CERTIFICATE OF ACCREDITATION

Pursuant to Section 353 of the Public Health Service Act (42 U.S.C.263a) as revised by the Clinical Laboratory Improvement Amendments (CLIA), Public Law 110-578, the above named laboratory located at the address shown hereon (and other locations registered under this certificate) is hereby authorized to accept human specimens for the purposes of performing laboratory examinations.

This certificate shall be valid until the expiration date above, but is subject revocation, suspension, limitation, or other sanctions for violations of the Act or the regulations promulgated thereunder.

John J. Sullivan, Director
Division of Laboratories and Acute Care Services
Survey and Certification Group
Center for Medicaid and State Operations

✔ Is issued under the name "Department of Health and Human Services—Health Care Financing Administration"

✔ Lists the name and address of the lab

✔ Lists the name of the lab director

✔ Contains the lab's CLIA ID#

✔ Clearly identifies the type of certificate

✔ Indicates the expiration date for the certificate

✔ Is signed by an authorized HCFA representative

Private Accreditation Agencies

As mentioned earlier, laboratories performing moderate-to-highly complex tests must be certified through the HCFA. Laboratories have the choice to apply for either a CLIA Laboratory Certificate of

Compliance or a CLIA Laboratory Certificate of Accreditation. If the lab chooses to apply for a CLIA Laboratory Certificate of Accreditation, the laboratory will not be inspected by the State Department of Health, but by a Private Accreditation Agency. The Private Accreditation Agency must be approved by the HCFA, which means that the HCFA has deemed the accreditation program to meet CLIA statutory requirements.

The following is a list of private agencies that have been approved by HCFA:

✔ Joint Commission on Accreditation of Healthcare Organizations (JCAHO)

✔ American Osteopathic Association (AOA)

✔ American Association of Blood Banks (AABB)

✔ College of American Pathologists (CAP)

✔ Commission on Office Laboratory Accreditation (COLA)

✔ American Society of Histocompatibility and Immunogenetics (ASHI)

Other than CLIA certificates, CAP certificates are the ones most commonly provided. It can take up to six months for CAP to issue an accreditation certificate. When CAP certifies a lab, it notifies HCFA. HCFA then issues a CLIA Laboratory Certificate of Accreditation.

CLIA Exemptions

HCFA recognizes somes states as having equal or more stringent laws than CLIA. Labs that are licensed in the following states are exempt from CLIA requirements.

✔ New York is partially exempt. While commercial laboratories and hospital laboratories are not required to be CLIA certified, private physician office laboratories are required. Therefore, New York is partially exempt from CLIA. For example, if an Investigator in New York is performing a urine pregnancy test required per protocol, the Investigator must have a CLIA Laboratory Certificate of Waiver.

✔ Washington

Veterans Administration (VA) Medical Centers are also exempt from CLIA.

CLIA waives certification requirements for the following situations because they do not treat subjects based on the lab results:

✔ Any laboratory that conducts testing solely for forensic purposes.

✔ Research laboratories that test human specimens, but do not report any patient-specific results for the diagnosis, treatment, or assessment of the health of individual patients.

✔ Individuals who assist patients in their home with testing kits approved by the FDA for personal use (for example, home health agency employees).

✔ Entities that serve as collection stations for specimens, but send specimens to a certified lab for analysis.

Documentation of the proper laboratory license and certifications are critical to the conduct of a clinical trial at a site.

VI. The Creation of Study Source Documents

Documentation of clinical research projects is undeniably one of the most important aspects of conducting a clinical study; yet, it is one of the major deficiencies repeatedly found by FDA auditors. A common source of disagreements about what constitutes source documentation continues to be an ongoing dialogue between sponsors'/CROs'/SMOs' monitors and site personnel. Source documents confirm that the data were accurately reported and that the study was conducted according to the Protocol.

The International Conference on Harmonization (ICH), the Code of Federal Regulations, and GCP require the following:

1. written, informed consent by all subjects **prior** to the implementation of any study-related procedures; and

2. accurate, complete, and appropriate clinical research documentation.

A. Source Documents—What Are They?

The first recording of any observations made or data generated about a study subject during her/his participation in a clinical trial is source documentation. Source documentation is the foundation of all clinical studies. Source documents confirm the completeness and accuracy of data collection and show evidence that the study was conducted not only according to the protocol, but also ethically.

CFR 312.62 (b) states: "An investigator is required to prepare and maintain adequate and accurate case histories that record all observations and other data pertinent to the investigation on each individual administered the investigational drug or employed as a control in the investigation. Case histories include the CRFs and supporting data including, for example, signed and dated consent forms and medical records, including, for example, progress notes of the physician, the individual's hospital chart(s), and the nurses' notes."

ICH GCP 1.52 states: "Source documents are the original documents, data, and records (e.g., hospital records; clinical and office charts; laboratory notes; memoranda; subjects' diaries or evaluation checklist; pharmacy dispensing records; recorded data from automated instruments; copies or transcriptions certified and verification of their accuracy; microfiches; photographic negatives; microfilm or magnetic media; x-rays; subject files; and records kept at the pharmacy, at the laboratories, and at medico-technical departments involved in the clinical trial)."

Copies of the CRFs *are not* source documents unless specifically identified by the sponsor. *The sponsoring pharmaceutical companies' CROs/SMOs have been providing clinical research sites with source documents that are study-specific.* While this helps the CRC, generally it is better to create source documents that are study-specific and to mirror the information in the CRFs and reflect the standard operating procedures at the site.

Anyone involved in the clinical study can create source documents. This may include, but is not limited to, the PI, the subinvestigators, the CRC, the floor nurse (if an in-patient study), the physical therapist, the data coordinator, and so forth. The pharmacist who records the dispensing of the study drug creates a source document. A research subject can create source documents when he or she completes study-specific diaries.

B. Source Document Examples

✔ A record release form with the subject's signature and date;

✔ completed and signed HIPAA consent, if applicable;

✔ letter of referral from the subject's primary physician to the PI for study screening;

✔ screening or intake forms;

✔ medical history, including demographic data and documentation of inclusion/exclusion eligibility;

✔ original, signed, and dated Informed Consent Form;

✔ amendments to the original Informed Consent Form, signed and dated;

✔ physical exam notes;

✔ progress notes;

✔ study-specific flow sheets;

✔ study-specific checklists;

✔ adverse event list;

✔ subject diaries;

✔ nurse's notes;

✔ Medication Administration Records (MARs);

✔ concomitant medication list;

✔ hospital admission and discharge summaries;

✔ correspondence to and from a study subject; and

✔ death certificate.

C. Types of Medical Reports
Generated While a Subject Is Enrolled in a Study

✔ Laboratory: serology, chemistry, hematology, microbiology, urinalysis;

✔ ECG reports;

✔ MRI/CT scan reports;

✔ radiology reports;

✔ pathology reports;

✔ transfusion records;

✔ hospital admission summaries; and

✔ hospital discharge summaries.

Source documents should be accurate and complete enough to permit the entire reconstruction of the data in the unlikely event of losing the CRF. Information pertinent to the subject's participation in the study should be included. Variables, such as safety data and essential effectiveness, will determine the outcome of the clinical trial and should be documented. Adverse events, treatment, and follow-up should be described well. All communication with the Sponsor/CRO/SMO regarding approved Protocol waivers or deviations should be noted. (The IRB should be notified in writing of any waivers or deviations from the approved Protocol.)

It has been reported by experienced CRCs that every hour spent with a study subject generally requires an additional hour spent documenting and completing paperwork associated with the interaction. Documentation should be practical, limited to the essential, easy to routinize, and standardized but flexible enough to include unusual circumstances.

D. Good Clinical Research Documentation Details

✔ There should be a record of every visit and conversation with the subject in the subject's clinic/study record.

✔ Electronic messages and facsimiles should be printed and filed in the site regulatory binder.

✔ Logs of procedures should exist.

✔ Records of calibration of study-required equipment, including temperature logs, should be kept and filed appropriately.

✔ Screening and recruitment logs (including computer-generated lists of potential study subjects) should be retained to demonstrate that inclusion/exclusion criteria were performed according to the Protocol.

✔ Site visit monitoring logs should be kept to document the purpose and frequency of the monitoring visit.

✔ Records of missing or unobtainable data required by the Protocol should be explained appropriately by a memo to the file, if applicable.

✔ If information must be added to a previous entry, it should be inserted and noted as a late entry or addendum at the end of the text in the medical chart. It should not be squeezed in between previously written notes.

✔ If data must be changed or clarified, the industry standard is to put a single line through the original entry, change the data, and initial and date the change.

✔ Any changes to the data should be evident in an audit trail. Explanations added to the progress notes may be required.

A source document is *always* a source document. It may seem a good idea to recopy a source document, instead of crossing out yet another entry and correcting it, *but* there is always the possibility of a transcription error. In addition, these and similar attempts to obliterate or destroy original data are *not* acceptable. To an auditor, these redactions may elicit suspicion. Is the motive fraud or neatness? Once redacted, the data is no longer a source document. ***If it is not documented, it did not happen!***

E. Source Documentation Suggestions

The *Compliance Program Guidance Manual* used by the FDA to audit an investigative site is an excellent resource for source documentation. That, along with the industry standard, provides the rationale for the following documentation to support CRF data:

Notation that written, informed consent was obtained and that the consent form was dated and signed by the subject (or the subject's representative, if applicable) prior to the performance of any study-related procedure. It is generally a good idea to also note the time at which informed consent was obtained. This will confirm that study-related procedures, such as laboratory samples, were obtained after informed consent was obtained. If an investigator's signature is required on the consent form, and the investigator did not sign on the same date that the patient did, make sure the actual date that the investigator signed the informed consent is used. Note in the source the reason for the later date. *Under no circumstances should a CRC enter patient's initials on the consent, or enter the date for the patient.* The patient should perform these tasks by her/himself.

Record the date of entry into the study, the Sponsor's Protocol number, and the subject number.

The subject's diagnosis and current physical status prior to the initiation of any study-related procedures should be noted. Include details of medical history, checking the inclusion/exclusion criteria.

Record current medications, as well as medications discontinued within the past 30 days. Review the Protocol to determine if there are restricted or excluded medications and the wash-out period required by the Protocol. It is a good idea to ask potential subjects to bring their actual pill bottles to the screening visit. This way you can be sure the medication information being provided by the subject is accurate.

Document the name and/or number of the study drug dispensed, as well as the dosing information. Note the total amount of study drug dispensed at subsequent visits; include the amount of study drug returned by the subject. If there is a discrepancy, note the reason for it.

For example:

> *Patient #1234 did not return study drug dispensed on 4/10/04, inadvertently discarded empty bottle. Patient instructed on the importance of returning study drug, even if the bottle is empty.*

Patient #4562 missed two doses of study medication while on vacation. Patient instructed on the importance of taking the study drug according to the directions.

Patient #0001 did not return unused study medication dispensed on 5/8/04. Sponsor was contacted and gave approval to dispense additional medication. Patient will return unused study drug at the next visit. Patient instructed on the importance of returning unused medication at each visit.

Patient #6534 was screened for Protocol NA#0099 today. Informed consent was obtained prior to the initiation of any study-related procedures. The patient did not have any questions regarding the study or the study requirements. The patient understands his/her role as a study participant. The patient meets inclusion/exclusion criteria. Next visit scheduled for 6/10/04.

Document the dates and results of study-specific evaluations and procedures. Any deviations from the Protocol must be documented and reported to the Sponsor and the IRB.

Record all adverse events and complaints noted by the subject during the study and for the appropriate time specified by the Protocol. Include the last dose of study drug taken by the patient and any medical intervention or action taken to treat the adverse event or complaint.

In study progress notes, record the subject's condition during and/or after treatment.

Note the final disposition of the subject and the subject's status at the time of study termination. This includes premature study termination. Make sure you note the reason for premature study termination. There is a difference between study drug termination and study termination. While a subject may be terminated from study drug treatment, the subject may not be terminated from the study. This is study- and Sponsor-specific.

The most frequent cause of disagreements between CRAs and CRCs is the adequacy of source documentation.

F. Meeting the Requirements of Source Documentation

✔ Study-specific labels attached to progress notes;

✔ Protocol-specific flow sheets;

✔ Protocol-specific checklists; and

✔ Protocol-specific templates created by the site or in some instances the Sponsor, to collect the data required by the CRF.

A discussion between the Sponsor and/or the CRO/SMO concerning their expectations regarding source documentation prior to the initiation of the study is essential. This will avoid problems in the future. It is a good idea to obtain written requests for any requirements that deviated from your site's standard operating procedures. In advance, evaluate the source documentation requirements, and evaluate the extent to which you can comply. Do not hesitate to negotiate what is acceptable to all parties concerned. Educate the medical record department about the importance of research records.

Document any violations and/or deviations from procedures specified by the Protocol and the reason. This represents changes made to the Protocol that have not been approved by the Sponsor or the IRB. Since they may affect risk to the research subject and will impact the integrity of the data, violations and/or deviations play an important part in Warning Letters issued by the FDA.

All allied health professionals involved in the conduct of clinical research are responsible for conducting research ethically. The complete, accurate, and thorough documentation of the research subject's participation in the Protocol enables the research site to demonstrate the requirements for GCP were fulfilled during the conduct of the research study.

G. Data Clarification and Adverse Event Reporting

Adverse Events

ICH guidelines define an Adverse Event (AE) as:

> Any untoward medical occurrence in a patient or clinical investigation subject administered a pharmaceutical product and which does not necessarily have a causal relationship with this treatment. An adverse event (AE) can therefore be any unfavorable or unintended sign, which includes abnormal laboratory results, symptom or disease temporally associated with the use of a medicinal (Investigational) product.

To prove to regulatory agencies that they are safe and effective, drugs undergo extensive testing. Adverse events are one aspect of this safety evaluation, and it is important that any adverse events that occur in a study are reported accurately and promptly.

Adverse events must be in *appropriate* medical terminology with sufficient information to ensure that the occurrence is accurately recorded so that it can easily be matched against a coding dictionary such as MedDRA, COSTATR, WHOART, or ICD9.

When an adverse event is recorded, the terms used must be unambiguous, in acceptable English (although Latin terms can be used), and *with no spelling errors.*

Most of the examples used in this chapter have been recorded from actual clinical trials and are used to illustrate problems encountered by Data Management when recording adverse events.

Common Problems

Two Conditions Reported as One Adverse Event

- ✔ Anxious and insomnia
- ✔ Rash, fatigue
- ✔ Dizziness, nausea
- ✔ Muscle ache and back pain
- ✔ Nausea and asthenia
- ✔ Leucocytosis and fever
- ✔ Disorientation/agitation

The conditions noted above are *different* adverse events and cannot be coded together. These conditions must be separated into two individual adverse events. For example: Anxious will be mapped to a dictionary term of anxiety, whereas insomnia will be mapped to insomnia. In the case of dizziness and nausea, dizziness will be mapped to a dictionary term of dizziness and body system Nervous System, but nausea will be mapped to a body system Digestive System. Nausea and vomiting must be split into two adverse events if the MedDRA dictionary is being used for coding.

Medical Abbreviations

The use of medical abbreviations must be done with care. Refer to a standard reference book, such as Neil M. Davis 8th Edition Medical Abbreviations. For example:

- ✔ "Worsening RA" could mean worsening rales or worsening rheumatoid arthritis.
- ✔ "Worsening of AP" may denote worsening acute pancreatitis, worsening appendicitis, or worsening arterial pressure.
- ✔ "Increased DM" can be taken to mean increased dermatomyositis, increased diabetes mellitus, or increased diastolic murmur.
- ✔ "CHF" as well as being the medical abbreviation of chronic heart failure, can also be Crimean haemorrhagic fever or congestive heart failure.
- ✔ "C.O.L.D." means chronic obstructive lung disease, not coryza (common cold).
- ✔ "LAH" refers to either left anterior hemiblock or left atrial hypertrophy.
- ✔ "CM" could mean common migraine, continuous murmur, or chondromalacia.

Truncated Words

Adverse event text should not be shortened.

✔ "FR left ankle" may be assumed to be fracture of the left ankle, but the abbreviation for fracture is incorrect and should be FS or #. For clarity it would be preferable to use the word FRACTURE.

✔ "FR" is a medical abbreviation for "fluid restriction" and "factional reabsorption" as well as father.

✔ Pleurit could have many possible interpretations: pleuritic pain, pleuritis, etc.

Laboratory Data

In the case of changes in biochemistry of the blood or in alterations in hematology parameters, it must be specified if there was a measured increase or decrease.

✔ "Calcium"   Increased calcium or decreased calcium?

✔ "LFTs"   Decreased liver enzymes or increased LFTs?

✔ "Hg"   Elevated hemoglobin or decreased hemoglobin?

✔ "↓ Platelets"   Reduced platelets

Symptom versus Medical Diagnosis

Provide a diagnosis instead of a list of symptoms.

✔ "Upper respiratory tract infection" rather than "runny nose," "sore throat," "hoarseness," "sinus problem," "fever," etc.

✔ "Diarrhea" is preferred to the symptoms of "loose liquid stools," "increased frequency," and "abdominal pain."

✔ "Cold" could refer to an upper respiratory chest infection or a feeling of being cold; the term should be made specific to the problem reported.

Modifiers

Some medical terms need additional information to more completely describe the adverse event being reported. For example:

✔ "Cirrhosis"   can pertain to brain, kidney, liver, lung, malarial, ovarian, pancreas, spleen, or stomach

✔ "Caries"   refer to either bone or tooth

✔ "Amputation"   can be surgical or traumatic

✔ "Abortion"	can be therapeutic or spontaneous
✔ "Fibrocystic Disease"	can be fibrocystic breast disease or cystic fibrosis
✔ "Herpes"	can be simplex or zoster
✔ "Kaposi's"	can refer to Kaposi's disease, Kaposi's sarcoma or varicelliform eruption
✔ "Stiffness"	can describe muscles or joints
✔ "Ulcer"	can refer to gastric, stomach, duodenal, skin, corneal, decubitis
✔ "Cramps"	can refer to muscle or abdominal
✔ "Edema"	can be dependent, ankle, tongue, pharynx, face, peripheral, etc.
✔ "Hemorrhage"	unless describing a generalized hemorrhage, the site of the hemorrhage should be recorded: gastrointestinal hemorrhage, gum hemorrhage, gastric hemorrhage, etc.
✔ "Reflux"	gastrointestinal or kidney
✔ "Hernia"	umbilical, inguinal, hiatal
✔ "Incontinence"	urinary, fecal, or stress

Infections

Record either the site of the infection or the organism involved.

- ✔ In the case of a respiratory tract infection note whether it is an upper or lower respiratory chest infection.

- ✔ Eye infections can be of several types and should be specified: conjunctivitis, iritis, keratitis, retinitis, scleritis, uveitis, or kearatonconjunctivitis.

- ✔ Ear infections can be divided into otitis media, otitis externa, otitis interna, etc., depending on the site.

Sore

The word "sore" means either a lesion or a feeling of soreness.

Language

Care should be given to the meaning of the word used on the Case Report Form (CRF), as the entry may not be obvious to the person later entering the database.

"Angina" is defined in medical dictionaries as pain. Commonly, angina is taken to mean angina pectoris, but the term could or should be queried to ensure that this is the correct adverse event.

In France, "angina" is used for tonsillitis, and staff has queried French sites to ensure that a tonsillectomy is the correct treatment for angina. In Europe, "hypotonia" and "hypertonia" are commonly used terms for hypotension and hypertension. Elsewhere, however, standard medical dictionaries use these terms to mean decreased or increased tension in any part of the body (for example, muscle hypotonia, arterial wall hypertonia, or oscular hypertonia). The meaning of the term used should be investigated to ensure the correct term is being used for the condition being reported.

Pain

Pain terms should specify a site where the pain is located. The use of the word "pain" alone is not enough information to allow for the proper coding of the adverse event.

"Chest pain" can be either muscle or cardiac pain, and the type should be specified.

Rashes

When reporting a rash be sure to include not only the type of rash, i.e., macular rash or erythematous rash, but also the location of the rash. This information may be important, especially in a dermatology study, or in a study where the study medication being used is known to possibly cause a rash.

Nonsense Words

Some adverse events reported using nonmedical words and phrases may be queried. The following words have actually been used when reporting an adverse event:

- ✔ "Eruptions"
- ✔ "Increase in peptic symptoms"
- ✔ "Heat waves"
- ✔ "Root fracture"
- ✔ "Relaxed bowels"
- ✔ "GIT gases"
- ✔ "Elevation"
- ✔ "Blushing groin"
- ✔ "Gastric juice"
- ✔ "Wants to stop smoking"

- ✔ "Erection"
- ✔ "Temperature"
- ✔ "Erections disappeared"
- ✔ "Patient complains of 'funny head'"
- ✔ "Urinalysis pH9"
- ✔ "Farsightedness"
- ✔ "Fogginess"
- ✔ "Odd feeling in head"
- ✔ "Elbow twist"
- ✔ "Urine color pink"
- ✔ "Pacing"
- ✔ "Desaturation"
- ✔ "Large occult blood"
- ✔ "Left shin in differential"
- ✔ "Broken ribbon"
- ✔ "Nervosity"
- ✔ "She feels like she has a cloud in her head"
- ✔ "Patient 100% noncompliant: medication eaten by her dog on return from surgery: dog slept for 3 days and made a full recovery with sequelae"
- ✔ "Increase in brightness of vision"
- ✔ "Unusually enhanced alcoholic effect"
- ✔ "Penile bend"
- ✔ "Hematological failure"
- ✔ "Speech"
- ✔ "Jar of the left ear"
- ✔ "Frozen"
- ✔ "Goat attack"
- ✔ "Jumping Heart"
- ✔ "Eye injury—attacked by bird"
- ✔ "Adenoid Vegetation"

H. Queries

The Data Clarification Process

For many Study Coordinators, the Data Clarification Process is one of the most troubling and time-consuming components of conducting clinical research projects.

Study Coordinators often believe that the number of queries generated during a clinical trial is a negative reflection of their work. In some instances this may be true, but not in the majority of instances. Queries are considered by most clinical research coordinators as a dreaded event. For the most part, queries are generated for many reasons, such as:

- ✔ Amendments to the protocol
- ✔ Changes in case report form design
- ✔ Statistical program changes
- ✔ Clarification regarding information contained on the case report form
- ✔ Providing incomplete data on a case report form
- ✔ Providing too much information
- ✔ Spelling errors

The query or data process for a clinical trial begins when the protocol and case report forms are designed and ends when all queries have been resolved and the database is locked in preparation for FDA submission. The process may vary from Sponsor to Sponsor and from project to project. However, the resolution of these queries is an intricate part of the clinical trial and are a critical component to the submission of the data collected during the clinical trial for presentation to the FDA.

The Data Process from Start to Finish

In order to understand the data process resulting in the generation of queries it is important to know exactly how the process works. The process may vary from project to project and from Sponsor to Sponsor, however it still results in the generation of queries. In addition, there is generally a specific time specified by the Sponsor to resolve these queries.

The following timeline is an example of how the data process typically works:

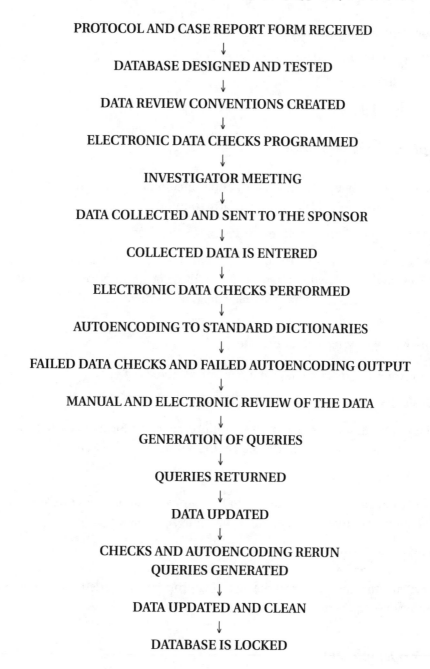

PROTOCOL AND CASE REPORT FORM RECEIVED
↓
DATABASE DESIGNED AND TESTED
↓
DATA REVIEW CONVENTIONS CREATED
↓
ELECTRONIC DATA CHECKS PROGRAMMED
↓
INVESTIGATOR MEETING
↓
DATA COLLECTED AND SENT TO THE SPONSOR
↓
COLLECTED DATA IS ENTERED
↓
ELECTRONIC DATA CHECKS PERFORMED
↓
AUTOENCODING TO STANDARD DICTIONARIES
↓
FAILED DATA CHECKS AND FAILED AUTOENCODING OUTPUT
↓
MANUAL AND ELECTRONIC REVIEW OF THE DATA
↓
GENERATION OF QUERIES
↓
QUERIES RETURNED
↓
DATA UPDATED
↓
CHECKS AND AUTOENCODING RERUN
QUERIES GENERATED
↓
DATA UPDATED AND CLEAN
↓
DATABASE IS LOCKED

I. Identify Data Problems

Report forms and routine monitoring visits may reduce the number of data problems that could be resolved during the completion of the case report form (CRF).

Most Common Data Offenders

1. Providing incomplete data
2. Providing too much data
3. Misspelling
4. Providing ambiguous data

The Incomplete Data Provider

✔ Frequently provides Adverse Event and Concomitant Medication Data without the required supporting information

✔ Leaves required boxes on the case report form pages unchecked

✔ Indicates procedures on the case report form as NOT DONE (ND) when a review of the source documents indicate the procedures captured in the source documentation have actually been performed

How to Work with the Incomplete Data Provider

✔ Look for questions that have not been answered.

✔ Explain data that is missing that is Not Done (ND).

✔ If appropriate, cross out, date, and initial case report form pages that will not be completed and explain the reason this information is not available.

✔ Look for boxes that are not checked.

✔ Verify the information contained in the source documents is consistent with the information recorded on the case report form pages.

✔ Provide start and stop dates for adverse events—indicate if they are ongoing or resolved. Document if treatment was given for the verifying the treatment and the dose if appropriate, recorded according to the Sponsor's requirements.

Providing Too Much Data

✔ Provides too much information for a single question

✔ Combines adverse events or medication on one line

✔ Provides investigator comments; while frequently providing extra information, these comments should be provided in a completely different place on the case report form

How to Work with the Investigator Providing Too Much Data

✔ Scrutinize the source documentation, especially the Medical History, Adverse Events, and Medication Pages for consistency.

✔ Verify adverse events, medications, medical history, and prior surgical procedures are recorded on a *separate* line of specific case report form page.

✔ Look for data on the case report form pages that do not belong on that specific page.

✔ Cross check Adverse Event pages with the medical history, current medical conditions, and medication page to verify the information on the case report form is accurate and complete.

✔ Verify there are no adverse events recorded that have been erroneously reported.

✔ Verify scheduled surgery has not been listed as an adverse event.

✔ Scrutinize the Medication Page of the case report form to ensure the start date of the medication that is the started at the time of the adverse event has been noted.

✔ Verify medical conditions documented at the beginning of the study on the Medical History case report form page have actually worsened since the start of the subject's participation in the study.

The Misspeller

✔ Places extra letters haphazardly

✔ Frequently spells words wrong

✔ Frequently uses symbols such as ↑↓;+; ≥; ≤; ± instead of the proper word

✔ Writes with moderate to severe illegibility, necessitating inquiry and clarifications

How to Work with the Misspeller

✔ Verify commonly misspelled words such as adverse events and medications to ensure they are spelled correctly.

✔ Clarify data that is illegible before it leaves the best person to decipher it, the author.

✔ Scrutizinize abbreviations to ensure the case report form guidelines allow for the use of abbreviations—if it is not a common abbreviation, it must be defined.

Ambiguous Data Provider

✔ Frequently provides symptoms rather than diagnosis

✔ Uses words like "fell," "pain," and "accident" to describe events, which need further clarification

✔ Supplies data requiring further clarification, i.e., "Ear Infection"—Is it Otitis Interna, Otitis Media, or Otitis Externia? Herpes—Simplex or Zoster? Diabetes—Mellitus or Insipidus?

How to Work with the Ambiguous Data Provider

✔ Look for terms that will need clarification: e.g., "fall," "pain," "accident," and "infection," "antibiotic," or "cold."

✔ Cross-check Adverse Event case report form pages with the Concomitant Medications and Medical History pages to find unreported adverse events.

✔ Know what medical terms can be coded.

✔ Verify the adverse events reported are valid.

✔ Verify start and stop dates for adverse events ("unknown" is not acceptable except on very rare occasions).

The objectives of completing the case report forms appropriately are:

✔ Quality of the data recorded is increased

✔ Increase the knowledge of the site's staff

✔ Decrease the number of queries

✔ Decrease stress for investigator, coordinators, monitors, and data managers

✔ Decrease late state project timelines

✔ Decrease the amount of work for the site's staff

✔ Decrease in project overruns

✔ Enabling safer drugs to be brought to market faster

VII. Obtaining Consents, Approvals, and Signatures

A. Obtaining Informed Consent

The law requires obtaining informed consent from each potential subject before that subject may participate in a clinical study or be screened for the study with clinical or laboratory procedures not normally carried out on similar subjects. The Code of Federal Regulations (21 CFR, Part 50, Subpart B) explains the details of informed consent.

The design and construction of an Informed Consent Form is the responsibility of the PI, but the Sponsor usually provides guidance in preparing the document and, possibly, the completed sample documents. In addition, the Informed Consent Form must be reviewed and approved by the IRB at each participating institution *before* it can be used.

One of the most important responsibilities of the CRC is to make sure that every potential subject (or that a subject's duly authorized representative) reads, understands, and signs an Informed Consent Form before participating in a study. Furthermore, the CRC must be sure that all signatures, dates, and other required information have been obtained.

The Informed Consent Form is designed to give the subject or a legal representative *easy-to-understand information* regarding the following aspects of the study:

✔ general design and purpose of the study;

- ✔ total length of the study;

- ✔ number of visits required for the study;

- ✔ total number of subjects in the study and number at the subject's particular site;

- ✔ benefits of the study treatment;

- ✔ risks of the study treatment;

- ✔ side effects associated with the study treatment;

- ✔ specified procedures unique to the study and risks involved;

- ✔ that the subject may receive a placebo and not active treatment (if applicable);

- ✔ alternative therapies that the subject may be offered;

- ✔ right of the subject to withdraw with no penalty;

- ✔ whom to contact 24 hours a day in case of questions or emergencies;

- ✔ confidentiality of subject records;

- ✔ costs and compensation; and

- ✔ compensation or medical treatments available for any research-related injury.

The rationale and basic content of informed consent have been set forth by FDA regulations. These regulations are described in the CFR, which may be obtained from the FDA (see Appendix I for contact information). While informed consent has traditionally been obtained by providing each subject with a written description of the elements of the study, some organizations are using novel approaches to educate prospective subjects. One of the most intriguing methods involves the presentation of the informed consent information in a video format, in conjunction with the written document. This approach is particularly useful for demonstrating difficult-to-explain procedures (such as cardiac catheterization, a novel surgical technique, and how to complete a patient diary), and gives the subject a visual opportunity to assess the risks and benefits associated with the study.

B. Obtaining Institutional Review Board Approvals

An IRB has at least five members with a diverse background of experience. The diversity of the IRB members' backgrounds will ensure cultural, educational, and racial diversity reflecting that of the local community. Members may include physicians, nurses, clergy, social workers, lawyers, and ethics experts. This enables the board to make an assessment of the validity of the study objectives. The Code of Federal Regulations (21 CFR) Part 56 reviews the regulatory considerations associated with IRBs.

Approval of a Protocol by the IRB is required in the following three situations. In each case, proper documentation for the approval is required.

Initial IRB Approval. Generally, initial review and approval by the IRB of the Protocol, the investigator, subinvestigators, the site(s), and the study site's Informed Consent Form and advertisement (if applicable) is required before enrollment can begin.

Until the investigator receives written IRB approval, no subject can undergo any procedures for the purpose of determining eligibility for the study.

Protocol Amendment IRB Approval. Should an amendment to the Protocol become advisable, in most cases, IRB approval must be received before the amendment can be implemented. In emergency situations, the amendment may be implemented first and the IRB notified within 10 days.

Continuing IRB Approval. Continuing IRB approval must be obtained for studies that last for more than one year, or other specified period. This will consist of documentation of the IRB's annual review and continuing approval of the Protocol.

Continuing IRB approval is obtained minimally on the annual anniversary date of the original approval and yearly thereafter, or as specified by the IRB, for as long as the study continues. The site may also be audited by the IRB to ensure the study is being conducted properly. If the IRB requires a fee, a note describing this fee (known as the "IRB Fee Letter") should be included in the Study File.

C. Reviewing the Protocol and Obtaining Signatures

Each clinical study must have a written Protocol, which is the document that gives specific instructions for the conduct of the study. Approval of the Protocol by the IRB must be obtained *before* any subjects are allowed to participate or are requested formally to consent to participate in the investigation.

In addition, the PI must submit significant changes or amendments to the Protocol to the IRB if such a change increases the risk to subjects or adversely affects the validity of the investigation or the rights of the subjects. The investigator must obtain approval by the IRB before such change or deviation is implemented. When the change is made to eliminate or reduce the risk to subjects, it may be implemented before the review or approval by the IRB. In these instances, the investigator is required to notify the IRB, in writing, of the change within 10 days after implementation.

All changes or revisions to the Protocol, and the reasons for those changes, must be documented, dated, and maintained with the Protocol.

Before the site initiation visit with the Sponsor, the investigators and CRCs must read the Protocol. They should highlight important topics and identify any questions that need clarification by the Sponsor or CRO/SMO.

D. HIPAA Regulations and Clinical Research

On April 14, 2003, the HIPPAA regulations went into effect as a federal law. HIPAA stands for The Health Insurance Portability and Accountability Act of 1996. HIPAA is a privacy rule providing federal protection for the privacy of protected health information. HIPAA also protects against the misuse of individually identifiable health information.

How HIPAA Will Affect Clinical Research

✔ Research subjects must sign a document that allows access to their protected health information necessary for the subject to participate in a clinical trial. Research sites will implement one of the following policies:

   1. Some Institutional Review Boards (IRBs) will use the Sponsor's HIPAA authorization form as a stand-alone document.

   2. Some IRBs will incorporate the required HIPAA language into the informed consent form.

✔ Current subjects in an active clinical trial, who have already signed an informed consent to participate in the active clinical trial will be grandfathered into the regulation and will not need to sign a revised informed consent or authorization form, unless directed by the research site's local IRB.

✔ Research subjects, who sign an informed consent document on or after April 14, 2003, must sign the revised informed consent document or an authorization form to allow the Sponsor's representative access to their protected health information.

✔ Clinical trials that had not been initiated on or after April 14, 2003 and all new clinical trials will have verbiage in their contracts confirming they will only enroll subjects in clinical trials willing to sign the authorization.

✔ HIPPAA will have an impact on research site selection and the prescreening of potential subject charts.

HIPAA Required Elements for Authorization

A HIPAA authorization form must contain the following required elements:

✔ description of the information to be used or disclosed in a specific and meaningful fashion;

✔ identification of the person(s) authorized to make the requested use or disclosure;

✔ identification of the person(s) to whom the covered entity may make the requested use or disclosure;

- ✔ description of the purpose or the use or disclosure;

- ✔ expiration date or event;

- ✔ signature of the individual and date (personal representative is allowed if description of representative's authority to act for the individual is provided);

- ✔ statement of the individual's right to revoke the authorization and that revocation must be in writing;

- ✔ statement of consequences of the individual's refusal to sign the authorization;

- ✔ statement of the potential for information to be redisclosed by the recipient and thus no longer protected by this subpart;

- ✔ statement of the individual's agreement to denial of access to personal health information (PHI) created or obtained for research purposes while the clinical trial is in process;

- ✔ authorization must be in lay language; and

- ✔ a copy of the signed authorization must be provided to the individual.

VIII. Pertinent Forms and Study Records

A. The Test Article Inventory System

The Test Article Inventory System will dictate where test articles are to be stored and who will keep track of the amount of test articles received, dispensed, and returned to the Sponsor. The inventory system must ensure that:

- ✔ adequate supplies are always on hand;

- ✔ test articles are stored securely and in the proper environment (e.g., the refrigerator);

- ✔ the Drug Accountability Record is properly maintained;

- ✔ there is agreement between the number of test articles received versus the number of test articles dispensed (as recorded on the Drug Accountability Record and CRFs) versus the number of test articles on hand;

- ✔ the dispensing record and the CRFs agree concerning the identification of subjects receiving the test article;

- ✔ the test articles have not expired or have not been recalled by the Sponsor; and

- ✔ all test articles returned by subjects are accurately counted and recorded.

The CRA will need access to the test article storage area during site visits to verify the status of the test article supply. While some site-specific SOPs may not allow CRAs into the drug storage area due to confidentiality issues, the CRA must be able to document that the test article is being stored according to the specific Protocol requirements.

B. The Drug Accountability Record

The PI or designee (typically the CRC) is responsible for dispensing and accounting for the test articles and for exercising Good Clinical Practices (GCPs) in monitoring these supplies. The dispensing and return of test articles must be entered promptly on the Drug Accountability Record. The Sponsor or CRO/SMO should supply this form.

Under no circumstances should the PI supply test articles to other investigators, study sites, or to nonstudy patients, nor should she/he allow the test articles to be used in a manner other than as directed by the Protocol.

Test articles returned by a subject must be entered on the Drug Accountability Record and set aside for return to the Sponsor. *They must not be redispensed to anyone—not even to the same subject. Note: Study drug returned must be stored separately from study drug not yet dispensed.*

At the termination of the study, or at the request of the Sponsor or CRO/SMO, the CRA will collect all remaining supplies, and the final Drug Accountability Record will be completed. These will then be delivered to the Sponsor. A copy of the Drug Accountability Record should be retained in the Study File. All manifests documenting shipments of test articles should be retained as well, along with copies of a Returned Goods Form, if provided.

During site visits, the CRA will typically be required to make a 100 percent source document verification of all dispensing and return data that appear on the Drug Accountability Record.

C. Case Report Forms

Case Report Forms provide for the orderly transfer of data from the study site to the CRO/SMO or Sponsor. CRFs are preprinted pages that allow the investigator or CRC to write in appropriate data regarding demography, efficacy, safety, medication use, and other aspects of the study. Therefore, it is of the utmost importance that data are entered properly and accurately on the CRF. Currently, at many sites there are data coordinators completing CRFs from the same documentation. These data coordinators work closely with the CRC in the completion of the CRFs.

The following guidelines should be followed when completing CRFs:

  ✔ All entries should be completed legibly using a *black* ballpoint pen or a typewriter.

  ✔ Only acceptable medical terminology and standard abbreviations should be used.

  ✔ Care should be taken not to write on any other forms placed on top of the CRF (written impressions will transfer to all copies of the carbonless forms underneath).

  ✔ Time should be entered as military time (a conversion chart is provided in Appendix IV, Part A).

  ✔ Numbers should be used to indicate dates (e.g., 10-01-02, not Oct. 1, 2002), unless otherwise specified.

  ✔ When completing the CRF and other documents pertaining to the study, there must be a response to every question so that the study data is complete for later entry into the Sponsor's database. Blank spaces, question marks, or zeros should not be used for unknown quantities. Instead, in cases where the data requested are unavailable, the following abbreviations can be used:

N/Av—not available. This abbreviation is used when the data are not available because they are not retrievable, the subject cannot remember, or the data were lost.

N/A—not applicable. This should be used for data that do not apply to the subject. For example, if the CRF calls for the date of the last pelvic examination and the subject is a man, "N/A" should be entered.

N/D—not done. This is entered when the data were not obtained. For example, if a vital sign such as blood pressure was requested but was not measured, enter "N/D."

Note: Sponsors may provide the site with a list of acceptable, study-specific abbreviations.

✔ Each item should be answered or checked individually rather than by using vertical lines or "ditto" marks to indicate a series of identical answers. The CRA needs to verify that the item was addressed.

Any discrepancies or missing data noted by the CRC or the CRA during site visits should be resolved before the data are forwarded to the CRO/SMO or Sponsor. A memo to file may be required to explain missing data or discrepancies, as well as deviations from Protocol.

Corrections should be made in the following manner:

✔ The original entry should be lined out with a single line drawn through the error so it remains legible (not erased, written over, or covered up by correction fluid).

✔ The correction should be entered in ink and initialed and dated by the person making the correction.

Only the PI or the designee listed on the Authorized Representative Signature Record (Site Signature Log) may enter corrections on original CRFs.

The CRA is responsible for inspecting every page of data before the CRFs are sent to the Sponsor or CRO/SMO. This inspection generally consists of a complete audit of all laboratory test values, the signed Informed Consent Forms, and critical nonlaboratory data (e.g., inclusion and exclusion criteria) against the source documents. In addition, a spot-check of at least 20 percent of all other data is typically performed. The CRA will also check for legibility, completeness, and consistency.

Before a review of the CRFs is conducted, the CRC should be sure that all forms are available, completed, and signed for the CRA's inspection within two weeks of study subject contact, and provide explanations for missing data (e.g., delayed laboratory reports).

The CRC is responsible for making sure that all CRFs have been dated and signed by either the PI or an associate named on Form FDA 1572. If an associate signs CRFs, the investigator must provide signed documentation that affirms his/her review and approval of the CRFs before their release to the CRO/SMO or Sponsor.

D. Authorized Representative Signature Record (Site Signature Log)

This record is maintained at each clinical study site to document the full name, handwritten signature, and initials of the PI and the representatives who are authorized to complete and/or make changes to the CRFs. A copy of this document should be maintained in the on-site investigator Study File.

If newly authorized representatives are assigned during the study, a new Authorized Representative Signature Record will be initiated for those signatures. This information should also be forwarded to the Sponsor.

E. The Adverse Experience Form

An adverse experience can be broadly defined as a medical complaint, change, or possible side effect of any degree of severity that may or may not be attributed to the test article. The reporting of adverse experiences is an extremely important part of conducting a clinical study, and the CRC plays a vital role in the proper and timely reporting of adverse experiences and their follow-ups.

The Adverse Experience Form included in the CRF packet provided by the Sponsor is used to record events that the investigator regards as adverse experiences (see Appendix II, Form 4). The investigator has the final decision regarding what is to be reported on the Adverse Experience Form, but the CRA may question the investigator about including unreported complaints found in the source documents or reported in other documents included in the CRF. If there is a question regarding where any study subject information is to be reported, the CRA should be contacted.

Some Sponsors list concomitant medications on Adverse Experience Forms because the event may be related to the concomitant medication and not the test drug.

Serious adverse experiences must be reported promptly to the Sponsor. A serious adverse event is defined as any adverse drug experience occurring at any dose that results in any of the following outcomes: death; a life-threatening adverse drug experience; in-patient hospitalization or prolongation of existing hospitalization; a persistent or significant disability/incapacity; or a congenital anomaly/ birth defect. An important medical event that may not result in death, be life-threatening, or require hospitalization may be considered a serious adverse drug experience when, based upon appropriate medical judgment, the event may jeopardize the patient and may require medical or surgical intervention to prevent one of the outcomes listed in this definition.

An adverse experience can meet the definition of serious adverse event and, ultimately, not be related to the study drug. In the event of a serious adverse experience, the Sponsor has 10 working days during which to file a Drug Experience Report via the MedWatch Form (see Appendix II, Form 5) to the FDA. The MedWatch Form is part of an overall program designed to streamline the reporting of adverse events and product defects associated with medications, devices, and nutritional products. These reports are essential to FDA drug surveillance efforts. MedWatch Forms can be obtained from the Sponsor or directly from the FDA (1-800-FDA-1088). To complete the MedWatch Form, the Sponsor will need the following information from the CRC:

✔ subject's initials, study number, age, and sex;

✔ adverse experience reported, all relevant tests and laboratory data, and the status of the reaction to date;

✔ dates of test article administration, from the first dose to the time of adverse experience;

✔ whether or not the test article was discontinued and, if so, whether the reaction stopped;

✔ whether or not test article administration was resumed and, if so, whether the reaction reappeared;

✔ whether or not the investigator believed the experience was related to the test article; and

✔ any other factors the investigator considers to be relevant (e.g., concomitant drugs, history, and/or diagnosis).

The PI is also obligated to report in writing serious adverse experiences to the IRB within *10* working days. Some IRBs will require a written report within 24 to 48 hrs. Make sure you review the IRB's reporting requirements.

Any abnormal laboratory values, abnormal clinical findings, or adverse experiences that the PI considers to be clinically significant must be medically managed until resolved. Follow-up information should be transmitted regularly to the CRA.

Note: If a patient dies while participating in a clinical trial, a copy of the death certificate may be required. Therefore, it is wise to obtain and have one in the CRC's files.

F. Specimen Handling and Submission Forms

The collection of biologic specimens for shipment to a reference-testing laboratory will be required by most Protocols. Common specimens include plasma, serum, urine, and tissue. The Protocol will provide specific methods for their collection, preservation, and shipping. The Sponsor will supply instructions for the identification and storage of these specimens as well as the necessary submission forms to be completed at the time of shipment.

It is the responsibility of the investigator and CRC to see that specimens are collected and stored as required by the Protocol. Labels and forms identifying the subject, type of specimens collected, site of collection, and date and time of collection are to be completed at the time of the procedure by the investigator or designee.

A complete review of specimen collection and handling procedures usually takes place with the investigator and staff before initiation of the study. In the event that the Sponsor is using a central laboratory, the central laboratory will provide the site's staff with a manual that is study-specific, including instructions for specimen collection and shipment.

G. The Subject Enrollment Form

The Subject Enrollment Form serves many purposes. It provides a checklist of the CRF documents to be completed for each visit and serves as a record of those components of the CRF that have been completed and submitted to the CRO/SMO or CRA. In addition, the Subject Enrollment Form is an aid in scheduling subject visits.

H. The Site Visit Log (Monitor Log)

The Site Visit Log (Monitor Log) is used to record visits made to the study site by the Sponsor's authorized representative, usually the CRA or a CRO/SMO representative. At each visit, the visitor will sign the Site Visit Log. This log must be kept in the Study File. Should the FDA audit the study, the FDA inspector will want to review the Site Visit Log to determine the frequency of site visits made by the Sponsor and the CRO/SMO, if applicable.

I. The Telephone Log

The Telephone Log is used to record all telephone contacts pertaining to the study. In addition to the date and time, the items discussed, action taken, and follow-up required should also be included. In some instances, the Sponsor will not require a site visit follow-up letter. In these cases, the CRA may contact the site after the visit to discuss the visit. Record this conversation in the Telephone Log; some CRAs will date and initial this telephone conversation as accurate during their next monitoring visit. As with the Site Visit Log, the Telephone Log should also be kept in the Study File. A sample Telephone Conversation Record is provided in Appendix II (Form 6).

J. Delegation of Authority Log

The Delegation of Authority Log is usually required for the purpose of identifying what study-specific tasks have been delegated by the PI. This is an ICH requirement.

IX. The Prestudy Site Visit

Before test articles can be sent to the study site and subject enrollment can begin, an initial site visit is conducted by a representative of the Sponsor and the CRO/SMO, if applicable. This is called the prestudy site visit. Sponsors are now utilizing the prestudy visit as a tool to ensure the facility is appropriate for study.

A. Site Initiation Visit

The purpose of this visit is to give the Sponsor's representative the opportunity to review the study documents, particularly the *Investigator Brochure*, Protocol, and CRFs, with the PI and staff. The *Investigator Brochure* is a document that summarizes everything known about the test article to date. One of its purposes is

to inform investigators of the pharmacologic events and side effects that have been observed in past studies. The Protocol gives specific instructions for the conduct of the study. During the prestudy site visit, the Sponsor's representative will discuss the Protocol and its CRFs page by page. In addition, the Sponsor's representative will outline study procedures; inspect the facilities; and verify safe, secure, and appropriate storage of the test article. A representative of the CRO/SMO involved in the study may also be a participant in this review.

At the conclusion of this visit, if everything has met the approval of the Sponsor, authorization to initiate the study may be given.

X. Recruiting and Enrolling Subjects

The first step in initiating the actual clinical study enrollment is to obtain a list of potential subjects. This can be accomplished by examining subject listings from various sources and by publicizing the study. Examples are given below.

A. Prospective Subject Groups

Lists of prospective subjects can be obtained from the following:

✔ charts in physicians' offices;

✔ computer printouts by diagnosis from hospital clinic records;

✔ support groups;

✔ group screening records;

✔ clinical laboratory screening records; and

✔ referrals from physicians, nurses, coordinators, and other specialty areas (e.g., radiology, laboratory), with a referral fee offered.

B. Methods of Publicizing the Study

A clinical study can be advertised or publicized in a variety of ways. However, IRB and Sponsor approval are required in advance for newspaper, radio, and television advertising and for any signs that are to be posted in public places, such as waiting rooms (see Appendix II, Form 7 for a sample sign). The following are several methods by which patients may learn about the availability of a clinical study:

✔ advertising (newspaper, radio, television);

✔ signs/posters for waiting areas;

✔ quarterly newsletter to subjects;

✔ billing statements;

✔ Kiwanis, Lions Clubs, Rotary Clubs, or other community groups;

- ✔ local churches and daycare centers;

- ✔ subject information in waiting rooms/examination areas;

- ✔ health fairs;

- ✔ local colleges and universities; and

- ✔ notices to local support groups for specific diseases.

Several states, including Florida, have enacted laws for advertisements by healthcare providers of free or discounted services. These laws require that specific language be included in study-related advertisements. To see if your state has enacted a law similar to the one enacted by the state of Florida, contact the appropriate agency in your state from which you may obtain this information. The following is the Florida Statute:

Florida Statutes Chapter 455.664

Advertisement by a Health Care Provider of Free or Discounted Services; Required Statement

In any advertisement for a free, discounted fee, or reduced fee service, examination, or treatment by a health care provider licensed under chapter 4 58, chapter 4 59, chapter 4 60, chapter 4 61, chapter 4 62, chapter 4 63, chapter 4 64, chapter 4 66, or chapter 4 86, the following statement shall appear in capital letters clearly distinguishable from the rest of the text:

THE PATIENT AND ANY OTHER PERSON RESPONSIBLE FOR PAYMENT HAS A RIGHT TO REFUSE TO PAY, CANCEL PAYMENT, OR BE REIMBURSED FOR PAYMENT FOR ANY OTHER SERVICE, EXAMINATION, OR TREATMENT THAT IS PERFORMED AS A RESULT OF AND WITHIN 72 HOURS OF RESPONDING TO THE ADVERTISEMENT FOR THE FREE, DISCOUNTED FEE, OR REDUCED FEE SERVICE, EXAMINATION, OR TREATMENT.

However, the required statement shall not be necessary as an accompaniment to an advertisement of a licensed health care provider defined by this section if the advertisement appears in a classified directory, the primary purpose of which is to provide products and services at free, reduced, or discounted prices to consumers and in which the statement prominently appears in at least one place.

Added by Laws 1997, c.97-261,x 81, eff. July 1, 1997

However, if the advertisement does not state "free" or "at no cost," the statement is not required. Check with your IRB for further clarification.

C. Presenting the Study to the Subject

Once a list of potential subjects has been obtained, the CRC must screen the subjects for acceptability and introduce them to the details of the study. This can be accomplished by telephone or in person.

When first contacting or meeting a potential study subject, the CRC should give his/her name and affiliation with the clinic or physician conducting the study. The reasons for conducting the current study should be explained, and an investigational drug study should be defined, if appropriate. That is, the subject should understand that the drug has been previously used in humans, but additional human data are needed before the drug may be introduced to the marketplace.

The subject is then screened according to the inclusion/exclusion criteria set forth in the study Protocol. If the subject meets the criteria, the CRC can outline the details of the study more fully.

The potential benefits and possible side effects of the study drug should be discussed. The subject should be made fully aware of the time commitment required, the need to administer the test article as instructed, the need to follow the Protocol, and the importance of compliance. The length of the study, the number of on-site visits needed, and the procedures that will be performed at each visit should be fully outlined.

If the subject has been contacted by telephone, an appointment should be made for him/her to come in to review and sign the Informed Consent Form. If the subject has been contacted in person, informed consent can be obtained at this visit. The subject must review the Informed Consent Form and then be encouraged to ask any questions regarding the study and informed consent. The subject then signs the form with the CRC acting as witness. (A duly authorized representative may act on behalf of the subject.) The PI's signature will also be obtained on this form.

Once informed consent has been obtained, the subject's next appointment (typically the baseline screening visit) should be scheduled. The subject should be given the CRC's name and phone number. The subject also receives a copy of the Informed Consent Form, any study overview, and a confirmation letter (see Appendix II, Form 9), if appropriate.

It is the responsibility of the CRC and investigator to ensure that a clinical study has been completed with the designated number of clinically acceptable subjects and that these subjects report for every scheduled visit. Therefore, when first presenting a study to a potential subject, it is important to point out the benefits of study participation. These might include the following key points:

✔ preferential treatment, including convenient appointment times, no delays getting in for a scheduled appointment, ample appointment time, confirmation calls for next visit, follow-up calls and letters, transportation provided if needed, personalized appraisal of laboratory test results, and thorough healthcare;

✔ free medical and laboratory tests (e.g., electrocardiogram, chest radiographs, and blood and urine analyses);

- ✔ possible monetary compensation for travel expenses;
- ✔ opportunity to participate in innovative drug research;
- ✔ opportunity to possibly help others; and
- ✔ opportunity to increase understanding about disease processes.

To ensure fair balance, the subject must also be made aware of the potential risks involved in participating in the study.

On occasion, a subject will require special instructions about a particular procedure or test. The following box provides an example of one such special information directive.

Instructions for 24-Hour Urine Collection

The same amount of liquids should be consumed during the collection period as are normally consumed. No alcoholic or caffeine-containing beverages (coffee, tea, cola) may be consumed during this period.

The collection starts **after** you empty your bladder in the morning. **(The urine voided at this time is not included in the collection.)** Write the time and date on the label of the specimen container. Collect all urine voided for the next 24 hours in this one container, including the first specimen voided the following morning.

The specimen container should be refrigerated during the collection period. Each voiding should be added to the container as soon as possible.

Proper collection and refrigeration of the urine specimen is very important for accurate test results. Please follow the above directions and call me if you have any questions.

[Name]
Clinical Research Coordinator

[Phone number]

XI. Conducting the Study and Keeping Records

A. Study Activities

All the work performed up to this point should facilitate the accurate and timely transfer of study data to the CRFs. However, while the clinical study is being conducted, the CRC must ensure that clinical findings and laboratory data are properly recorded. Toward this end, the CRC should:

✔ organize and label specimen containers;

✔ prepare all laboratory requisition sheets;

✔ prepare subject workfolders before each visit;

✔ oversee the receipt and handling of test articles and laboratory specimens;

✔ maintain all files, records, and logs; and

✔ prepare for site visits.

For a study to be successful, *the Protocol must be followed and subject numbers maintained.* Some common pitfalls to avoid follow.

Lack of Timely Treatment. This may occur, leading to subject withdrawal if the physician's office staff is not alerted to the status of a study subject. To avoid this problem, the names of study participants should be highlighted in the physician's appointment book.

Laboratory Specimens Not Analyzed. Laboratory specimens must be processed within a certain period of time to meet the requirements of the laboratory or the Protocol. If specimens are not processed in a timely manner, the Protocol may be violated or important laboratory data may have to be excluded. When possible, a back-up sample should be retained.

Subject Absence. Subjects must show up for the required number of office visits, as dictated by the Protocol. To minimize subject absence, the CRC should telephone or mail a postcard to remind the subject of the upcoming appointment.

B. Subjects Lost to Follow-Up

If a subject is continually absent for appointments, the CRC should try to contact him/her by phone or certified letter to determine any scheduling conflicts and, if possible, reschedule the missed appointments. If attempts at follow-up using the Informed Consent Form and/or Letters of Agreement fail to convince the subject to report for scheduled appointments, the subject must be withdrawn from the study. If this is the case, every attempt should be made to have the test articles returned to the study site. The dates the subject was contacted and the type of contact used should be recorded in the study documentation.

C. Withdrawing a Subject

A subject may be withdrawn (terminated) from a study for several reasons, including failure to follow the Protocol or having an adverse reaction to the test article. A subject may also voluntarily withdraw. In the event a subject is withdrawn, a final visit should be scheduled, and the Sponsor should be notified of the subject's withdrawal. The subject's randomization code should not be broken at this time except in the case of an emergency. Many study Protocols require follow-up to be continued for a specified period of time after a subject is withdrawn, regardless of the reason for withdrawal.

D. Site Visits During the Study

The study site will be visited several times by the CRA or representative of the CRO/SMO. The complexity of the study or the number of subjects enrolled will dictate the number of visits. In addition, the CRA will monitor the study site by telephone. At each telephone contact or site visit, the CRA will confer with the CRC and the PI regarding the progress of the study.

During a typical site visit, the CRA is required to perform the tasks that follow. A review of these items will help the CRC prepare for the CRA's site visit.

Sign Site Visit Log (Monitoring Log). All of the Sponsor's personnel must sign the log each day they visit the study site.

Inspect original, signed Informed Consent Forms. These must be available for all subjects enrolled since the CRA's previous site visit.

Inspect CRFs. Case Report Forms must be completed legibly using a black ballpoint pen or typewriter. They must be available for review within two weeks after the subject completes the study.

Inspect Applicable Source Documents. The CRA will check for:

- ✔ properly completed entries;
- ✔ consistency between CRFs (all laboratory data and at least 20 percent of all other entries will be checked against source documents; most studies involve a 100 percent quality control check);

✔ conformity with the protocol; and

✔ properly signed and dated CRFs (these must be signed by the PI or the authorized designee).

Inspect Test Article Storage Area. The CRA will require access to this area to ensure that:

✔ adequate supplies are on hand;

✔ test articles are being stored properly;

✔ the Drug Accountability Record is being properly maintained;

✔ there is agreement amongst a physical count of the test articles received versus the number of test articles dispensed (as recorded on the Drug Accountability Record and CRFs) versus the number of test articles on hand;

✔ there is agreement between the dispensing record and the CRFs regarding the identification of subjects receiving the test article; and

✔ all test articles returned by subjects have been accurately counted and recorded on the Drug Accountability Record.

Inspect Bioanalytical and Specimen Storage Area. The CRA will need access to this area to ensure that samples collected since the last visit have been properly collected, handled, and stored.

E. Closing the Study and Retaining Records

At the termination of the study or at the request of the Sponsor, the CRA or representative of the CRO/SMO will pick up all remaining supplies and the final Drug Accountability Record for transmittal to the sponsor. A copy of the Drug Accountability Record will be retained in the Study File.

Study Close-Out Checklist. At the close of a study, the CRC is required to:

✔ schedule a close-out meeting with the Sponsor;

✔ notify the IRB of close-out and submit a final report;

✔ submit a final report to the Sponsor;

✔ submit miscellaneous charges to the Sponsor;

✔ return or discard laboratory supplies;

✔ bind and store CRFs;

✔ return or discard unused CRFs;

✔ label and ship frozen specimens;

✔ complete and store audit file;

- ✔ request randomization information; and
- ✔ track disbursements and reconcile study finances with the Sponsor.

IRB Final Report. The IRB Final Report is submitted after all the subjects have completed the study. This is sent to the IRB, with a copy sent to the Sponsor.

Record Retention. Federal law requires that the PI retain all study records for two years following the NDA approval date. The Sponsor may request longer retention periods. If the application is not approved, or no NDA is submitted, the PI must retain all study records for at least two years after the FDA has been notified that all clinical investigations of this indication have been discontinued. The ICH guidelines recommend that the records be retained for 15 years. When archiving study records, clearly label the following:

- ✔ Protocol number;
- ✔ Sponsor name;
- ✔ investigator name;
- ✔ investigator address; and
- ✔ study close-out date.

The PI must obtain the written consent of the Sponsor before disposing of any study records.

Subject Follow-Up. Subjects appreciate receiving correspondence after a study has been completed. You may wish to send them a letter describing the drug group in which they participated, you may provide a self-assessment form so they may rate their satisfaction with the conduct of the study, or you may wish to thank them for their participation.

XII. Preparing for an FDA Audit

A. FDA Inspections of Clinical Trials

The FDA Bioresearch Monitoring Program involves site visits to PIs, research Sponsors, CROs/SMOs, IRBs, and nonclinical (animal) laboratories. All FDA product areas such as drugs, biologics, medical devices, radiological products, foods, and veterinary drugs are involved in the Bioresearch Monitoring Program. The program procedures are dependent upon the product type. The objective of all FDA inspections is to ensure the integrity and quality of data and information submitted to the FDA, as well as the protection of human research subjects.

The FDA carries out three distinct types of clinical trial inspections:

- ✔ study-oriented inspections;
- ✔ PI-oriented inspections; and
- ✔ bioequivalence study inspections.

Study-Oriented Inspections

FDA field offices conduct study-oriented inspections based on assignments developed by headquarters staff. Assignments are based almost exclusively on studies that are important to product evaluation, such as NDAs and product license applications pending before the FDA.

When a PI who has participated in the study being examined is selected for an inspection, the FDA investigator from the FDA district office will contact the PI to schedule a mutually acceptable time for the inspection.

Upon arrival at the site, the FDA investigator will show FDA credentials, consisting of a photo identification, and present a Notice of Inspection Form to the PI. Food and Drug Administration credentials let the PI know that the FDA investigator is a duly authorized representative of the FDA.

If, during the course of an FDA inspection, a PI has any questions that the FDA investigator has not answered, either the director of the district office or the center that initiated the inspection may be contacted. The name and telephone number of the district director and the specific center contact person are available from the FDA investigator.

B. Types of FDA Inspections

There are two main types of FDA inspections that you are likely to encounter: a routine inspection and a for-cause inspection.

A *routine* inspection is conducted for those studies that are crucial to a product's evaluation and approval. For example, the studies may be pivotal to an NDA pending before the FDA. As the name would imply, a *for-cause* inspection is conducted when the FDA has a specific reason (cause) for inspecting a study site. The reason might be one of the following: (1) an investigator has participated in a large number of studies; (2) an investigator has done work outside his/her specialty; (3) the safety or efficacy results of an investigator are inconsistent with those of others conducting the same study; or (4) the investigator claims too many subjects with a specific disease or indication compared with the low numbers associated with his/her practice. Numerous other reasons determined by the FDA may trigger a for-cause inspection.

Before an inspection, the FDA will contact the PI, usually through a letter, to schedule the date of inspection and to determine the specific material to be audited. After receiving notice of a pending inspection, the PI should immediately contact the CRA because the Sponsor may wish to meet with site personnel prior to the FDA inspection.

The FDA inspector will present FDA credentials and a completed Form FDA 482, Notice of Inspection. (This form can be located on the FDA Web site.) The CRC should reserve a private area for the inspector, such as a conference room, and organize all appropriate source documents for the inspection. The inspector should have access to all, and only, the study data that was specifically requested, nothing more and nothing less. In addition, the following related information should be available:

- ✔ physicians' office records;
- ✔ hospital records;
- ✔ laboratory test results;
- ✔ subject medical history;
- ✔ subject follow-up data; and
- ✔ appointment calendar.

The inspector may also request the following information:

- ✔ the degree of delegation of authority by the PI;
- ✔ how and where data were recorded;

✔ how test article accountability was administered and maintained;

✔ how the Sponsor communicated with the PI and evaluated the study program; and

✔ certification of service/calibration for study-related equipment.

C. Parts of the Investigation

The investigation consists of two basic parts. The first is determining the facts surrounding the conduct of the study, including:

✔ who did what during the conduct of the clinical trial;

✔ the degree of delegation of authority performed by the PI— whether or not they were properly supervised and had the experience to do the assigned task;

✔ where specific aspects of the study were performed;

✔ if they are listed in the FDA 1572;

✔ how and where the data were recorded;

✔ how test article accountability was dispensed and maintained;

✔ how the CRA communicated with the clinical investigator; and

✔ how the CRA monitor evaluated the progress of the clinical trial.

Second, the clinical trial data is audited. The FDA investigator compares the data submitted to the FDA and/or the Sponsor with all available records that might support the data. These records may come from the physician's office, hospital, nursing home, central and/or local laboratories, and other sources. The FDA may also examine patient records that predate the study to determine whether or not the medical condition being studied was, in fact, properly diagnosed and whether or not an interfering medication had possibly been given before the study began. The FDA investigator may also review records covering a reasonable period after completion of the clinical trial to determine if there was proper follow-up, and if all signs and symptoms reasonably attributable to the product's use had been reported.

Principal Investigator-Oriented Inspections

A PI-oriented inspection may be initiated because a PI conducted a pivotal study that merits in-depth examination because of its singular importance in product approval or its effect on medical practice. An inspection may also be initiated because representatives of the Sponsor have reported to the FDA that they are having some difficulty getting case reports from the PI, or that the FDA has some other concern with the PI's work.

In addition, the FDA may initiate an inspection if a subject in a study complains about the Protocol or human subject's rights violations.

Principal investigator-oriented inspections may also be initiated because:

✔ the PI participated in a large number of studies;

✔ the PI enrolled a significantly large number of subjects into a Protocol;

✔ the PI participated in clinical trials outside of his/her specialty areas;

✔ the safety or effectiveness findings were inconsistent with those of other PIs studying the same test article;

✔ too many subjects with a specific disease given the locale of the investigations were claimed; and/or

✔ the laboratory results were outside the range of expected biological variation.

Once the FDA determines that a PI-oriented inspection should be conducted, the procedures are essentially the same as in the study-oriented inspection, except that the data audit goes into greater depth, covers more case reports, and may cover more than one study. If the investigator has repeatedly or deliberately violated FDA regulations or has submitted false information to the Sponsor in a required report, the FDA will initiate actions that may ultimately decide that the PI is not to receive investigational products in the future.

Bioequivalence Study Inspections

A bioequivalence study inspection differs from the other inspections in that it requires participation by an FDA chemist or a PI who is knowledgeable about analytical evaluations.

D. Preparation and Instructions for an FDA Audit

The Principal Investigator is responsible for *all* aspects of the clinical trial.

When arranging a Routine Audit of a site, the FDA will generally contact the site by telephone two to three weeks in advance to schedule a time and date that is convenient.

In a For-Cause Audit conducted by the FDA (including audits of Sponsors, CROs), the FDA generally will show up unannounced.

Prior to the FDA Audit

The Principal Investigator and his/her staff generally meet to discuss the audit and to organize the information and records requested by the FDA inspectors.

The following items should be available *before* the FDA inspectors arrive:

- ✔ Original, signed informed consent forms for all subjects, including those randomized as well as screen failures, including all signed versions of the informed consent

- ✔ Completed Case Report Forms (CRFs) for all subjects randomized, as well as screen failures

- ✔ Source documents and any other subject charts, including medical charts, laboratory reports, radiology reports, EKGs, etc.

- ✔ All versions of the Investigator Brochure

- ✔ All versions of the Protocol and Protocol Amendments

- ✔ All study drug receipt records, dispensing records, return records

- ✔ Complete and current Regulatory Binder

The FDA Audit

Upon arrival the of the FDA Inspector, request identification and obtain a business card or record his or her Name, Title, Division Office, and Contact Number. The FDA inspector will present a Form FDA 482 (Notice of Intent to Audit), which presents the clinical trial to be audited and the scope of the audit. It is important to identify a room or office for the FDA inspector to work in while conducting the audit.

Pointers
The following pointers may be helpful to remember during the FDA audit:

- ✔ Use the same room throughout the audit.

- ✔ Ensure the room has a telephone.

- ✔ Provide *only requested* clinical trial records.

- ✔ Ensure there are no records for any other clinical trial in the room designated as the room for the FDA inspector.

- ✔ If there are any cabinets, drawers, or cupboard in the room, ensure they are locked.

- ✔ Periodically check with the FDA inspector during the audit, instead of remaining in the room during the audit.

- ✔ Designate a contact person who can address questions, provide administrative support, track all requests from the auditor, and make photocopies, if appropriate.

- ✔ Document the records requested by the FDA auditor, the questions asked and the answers provided, as well as the name of the person providing the answers.

✔ Ensure the FDA auditor is escorted by site personnel at *all times* during the audit.

✔ Remember, the policy for FDA inspections, as well as Sponsor audits, is set by the Principal Investigator or the written Standard Operating Procedures (SOPs) in place at your site.

✔ Notify the medical records department and pharmacy if applicable and any other administrative offices.

✔ Notify the Institutional Review Board prior to the audit.

Be prepared to discuss the following items in detail:

✔ The informed consent process, including the person(s) responsible for obtaining written informed consent from the subject.

✔ The process for recruiting patients for the clinical trial.

✔ Delegation of responsibilities by the Principal Investigator.

✔ The CRF completion process.

✔ Serious Adverse Event (SAEs) reporting process and the reporting requirements for the Institutional Review Board (IRB).

✔ How the Principal Investigator maintains his/her oversight of the clinical trial.

✔ Concurrent clinical trials.

✔ Subjects who have discontinued the clinical trial being audited and subsequently may have been enrolled into another clinical trial.

✔ If an extension study is being audited, be prepared to provide the informed consent for the parent clinical trial for all subjects that have entered the extension study (the FDA auditor may only be verifying the subject signatures).

✔ Frequency of monitoring visits and how long the monitor stayed at the site during each visit.

✔ Study drug randomization and kit/bottle assignments.

✔ If an automated drug randomization process was used, ensure all related documents are available (including fax confirmations).

✔ Study drug accountability including overall and individual subject records.

✔ Ensure the area where the study drug is being stored is secure (locked) and there is limited access to the area.

✔ Ensure study drug not dispensed is being kept separate from study drug that has been returned/dispensed.

✔ Document any study drug discrepancies, including study drug containers inadvertently discarded by the patient.

✔ Ensure there is written documentation for the process of transporting study drug from one center to another, if applicable.

When the audit has been completed, the FDA auditor may issue the following documents:

✔ Form FDA 483 (Inspectional Observations) used for violations of the Federal Regulations. A Form FDA 483 is not always issued when the FDA conducts an audit; however, it is difficult *not* to get one.

✔ Establishment Inspection Report (EIR).

The Exit Interview

Appoint one person to provide comprehensive documentation of the information from the FDA auditor's Exit Interview with the Principal Investigator. The person designated should not be distracted by participating in the discussion. Remember tape recorders and video tape recorders are not permitted. The following information should be documented:

✔ Document each observation provided in the Form FDA 483.

✔ Make sure the observation is understood.

✔ Point out any deficiency noted in the observation that has been corrected since the beginning of the FDA audit (perhaps the observation will be deleted from the Form FDA 483, but that is not always likely).

✔ If the corrected observation has not been deleted from the Form FDA 483, request that the FDA auditor's Form FDA 483 and EIR include the fact that the observation noted has been corrected.

✔ If any observation noted deals with not meeting FDA regulations, *carefully* point out that the regulations are subject to interpretation, and, if correct, that "our interpretation was intended to provide the greatest protection to our patients."

✔ If it is clear that corrective action is necessary on an observation, and it is clear what the action to be taken is, indicate that you plan to take appropriate corrective measures on that observation immediately.

✔ *Do not commit yourself* to a future action that you do not intend to make or cannot undertake.

✔ If the corrective action is underway, but not completed with respect to a noted observation, report that fact to the FDA auditor.

✔ If you believe a noted observation is clearly not warranted, you should also point that out in a diplomatic manner.

✔ Set the proper tone.

✔ Be aware of your rights and protect them.

✔ Being argumentative will not be constructive and could make things worse.

✔ The primary focus is to clearly understand the observation(s) and address the observation(s).

✔ Do not be upset or offended if you do receive a Form FDA 483.

✔ If you respond within 10 working days of receipt of the Form FDA 483, your response will become part of the original report that is provided upon request of that report through the Freedom of Information Services (FOI).

✔ Remember, Form FDA 483 and EIRs are requested by Sponsors and CRO routinely.

General Advice

A few tips to make the process less painful:

✔ The more cooperative and the better prepared you are, the faster and more smoothly the inspection will proceed.

✔ Only answer the questions asked—*do not volunteer* any additional information.

✔ Do not be afraid to say "I don't know, but I will find out and get back to you," then do so—promptly.

✔ If you are not sure how to answer a question, say "I will have to get back to you on that," then obtain the appropriate advice on how to answer the question.

✔ If you don't feel comfortable answering a question, say "I will have to get back to you on that," then obtain appropriate advice on how to answer the question.

✔ Do not refuse to answer any question or provide anything; if you are not comfortable or cannot or do not want to answer the question, say, "I'll have to check with Dr. Z regarding that request."

✔ Try not to be overly friendly—remember what they are there to do; they may interpret your actions differently than you intended them.

✔ Know what you are talking about *before* you say anything and can back it up with documentation.

✔ You are free to call the Sponsor or CRO with any questions or concerns at any time during the inspection process (it is important to stay in close contact with the Sponsor/CRO).

✔ Remember, at the close-out visit for each of your studies make sure you keep the project contact information. Clients should provide the names and telephone numbers of contacts to be called after the site receives the initial call from the FDA or other Regulatory Authority.

✔ Regulatory Authority inspections occur most frequently from six months to up to two years following an NDA, BLA, or MAA (Marketing Approval Application) submission.

Summary

It is important to have written policies and procedures (Standard Operating Procedures—SOPs) in place for handling any FDA and Client/CRO audits/inspections:

✔ Make sure all staff members know how to handle such audits and that they have been trained in the SOPs.

✔ Make sure training records for your staff members are current and accurate.

✔ Be courteous at all times.

✔ When or if it is appropriate, request a teleconference with the inspector/auditor's supervisor.

✔ Be sure you understand all observations and findings.

✔ Answer all questions briefly, concisely, and truthfully (don't ever think the auditor/inspector will not find out the real answer).

✔ Visit FDA Web sites to read warning letters for Sponsors, Investigators, and Ethics Committees (there are several Web site addresses in this handbook).

E. Common FDA Inspection Findings

At the end of an investigation, the FDA investigator will conduct an "exit interview" with the clinical investigator. During this interview, the FDA investigator will discuss the findings from the inspection with the PI. The FDA investigator will clarify any misunderstandings that might exist, and may issue a written Form FDA 483 (Notice of Observations) to the PI. Following the inspection, the FDA field investigator will prepare a written report and submit it to headquarters for evaluation.

Once the report has been evaluated, the FDA headquarters usually issues a letter to the PI. The letter is generally one of three types:

Notice that no significant deviations from the regulations were observed.
This letter does not require any response from the PI.

Informational letter that identifies deviations from the federal code of regulations and GCP. This letter may or may not require a response from the PI. If a response is requested, the letter will describe what is necessary and provide a contact person for clarification or further questions.

Warning letter that identifies deviations from the code of federal regulations requiring prompt correction by the PI. This letter will provide the PI with a contact person for clarification and questions. In these cases, the FDA may inform both the Sponsor and the reviewing IRB of the deficiencies. The FDA may also inform the Sponsor if the PI's procedural deficiencies indicate ineffective monitoring by the Sponsor. In addition to issuing these warning letters, the FDA may take other courses of action, which may include regulatory, legal, and/or administrative sanctions.

Office for Human Research Protections

In June 2000, the FDA announced the creation of a new office at the Department of Health and Human Services, the Office for Human Research Protections (OHRP), to lead efforts for protecting human subjects in biomedical and behavioral research. This office replaces the Office for Protection from Research Risks (OPRR), which was part of the National Institutes of Health. The OPRR had authority over NIH-funded research.

According to the HHS Assistant Secretary, this new office will have increased resources and broader responsibility to ensure that patients taking part in research are better protected and fully informed. Everyone in the research community must share the responsibility for protecting research subjects. Medical research today is exploding with opportunity; however, to achieve the benefits of that research, we need a solid foundation of thoughtfully designed and thoroughly executed research-patient protection. This new OHRP will work with HHS agencies, research institutions, and Sponsors of research to ensure that this foundation is in place and working productively.

For additional information, a copy of the FDA *Compliance Program Guidance Manual* for Clinical Investigator Inspections (Program 7348.811), the document issued by the FDA investigator to conduct the inspection, is available by writing to:

Freedom of Information Staff (HFI-30)
Federal Food and Drug Administration
5600 Fishers Lane
Rockville, MD 20857

In addition, see the FDA information sheet, "Clinical Investigator Regulatory Sanctions," available at the FDA Web site.

F. Common Problems Identified in Audits of Clinical Trials

Audit Problem Areas	Items for Caution
Protocol	Under what Protocol date did the site initiate the study? If there are several versions, is the initiation version at the site and is it documented that this is the appropriate Protocol version? In addition, are all versions of the Protocol in the Investigator File?
Protocol Signature Page	Are corresponding completed signature pages provided for all versions of the Protocol?
Investigator Brochure (IB)	What version of the IB was provided to the site? Was the IB revised during the clinical trial? Is there documentation showing that the IB was received by the site (e.g., a memo to the Investigator File stating when the document was sent or a monitoring report listing the document as being at the site)? Where is the IB kept? If it is not kept in the Investigator File, is there a memo stating where at the site the IB can be located?
Form FDA 1572	Has the form been correctly completed, signed, and dated? If there is more than one form with the same signature/date, which form is correct? Has section #8 been appropriately completed? If Form FDA 1572 has been revised, was a copy sent to the IRB as well as the Sponsor?
Curriculum Vitae (CV)	Does the site have a CV for each person listed on FDA Form 1572? Does the site have a current medical license for the PI (some Sponsors require a copy of the medical license for the subinvestigator(s) as well as the PI)? Are all CVs current within two years? Can this be easily determined by review of the CV? Does the CV document the PI's affiliation with the site conducting the clinical trial?
Confidentiality Agreement	Was the Confidentiality Agreement obtained prior to the release of all study-related documentation (e.g., protocol, IB, Financial Disclosure form)?
Informed Consent Forms	Is there a copy of the IRB approved consent on file? Does the IRB documentation indicate that it is approving the consent? Has the informed consent been revised? Was the revised consent forwarded to the IRB? Is there documentation indicating that revised consent was approved? Have the patients participating in the Protocol signed the correct version of the informed consent? Are all sections of the informed consent signed and dated appropriately? If the site has foreign-speaking patients, is there a copy of the translated IRB approved consent? Has a certified translator completed the translation? Is there a back translation showing exactly what information is being presented to the patient? If the study has enrolled minors, is guardian consent obtained? If appropriate, is there assent by the minor participating in the Protocol? If there is another individual signing for the patient (e.g., daughter signs for father or wife signs for husband), is the individual the legal representative of the subject? If this is an in-hospital clinical trial, has the hospital's requirements for a legal representative been met? Has the reason there is another individual signing the informed consent for the patient been documented? Have all informed consent documents been signed prior to the initiation of any study-related screening procedures (e.g., medication wash-out periods, fasting for screening laboratory tests)?
Serious Adverse Events	Have all serious adverse events been reported to the Sponsor, CRO/SMO, and IRB within the specified time frames? Does the documentation provide a complete picture of the event? Has the condition been followed until resolution? In the event the patient has died, is there a copy of the death certificate in the source documents?
Institutional Review Board (IRB)	Does the site have documentation that the IRB is appropriately formed (e.g., membership list or assurance number)? Can all IRB approvals be easily tracked to the corresponding study document? Are there periodic reviews being appropriately submitted to the IRB and in a timely fashion? Is there documentation in the Investigator File from the IRB in response to the reviews? Are study summaries sent to the IRB upon study completion? Are all serious adverse events being appropriately reported? Are significant Protocol departures being reported to the IRB? Is there documentation in the Investigator File from the IRB in response to the reports?

Audit Problem Areas	Items for Caution
Site Visit Follow-Up Documentation	Are issues identified during a site-monitoring visit followed up in subsequent visits? Is there documentation to indicate that identified issues have been appropriately resolved?
Laboratory Documentation	Does the site have the appropriate laboratory certification (e.g., CLIA, CAP, and state license where applicable)? Does the certification cover the duration of the study? Are there normal laboratory value ranges available? If a central laboratory is being used for the study and there were Protocol samples sent to a local laboratory, is the appropriate certification for both the central and the local laboratories available in the Investigator File?
Investigational Supplies	Can all investigational supplies be accounted for? Are all study-related supplies being appropriately stored (e.g., if test articles need refrigeration, are they stored in a refrigerator with a temperature monitor and log? Is the temperature log current? If the test article is a controlled substance, have the appropriate guidelines for storage and dispensing been performed?)
Site Equipment Specific to the Protocol	Has the equipment being used been serviced recently? Are the service logs available? If calibration is required, has the calibration been performed prior to the initiation of any study-related procedures? Is there documentation of the calibration?
Correspondence	Is there sufficient correspondence between the site and the Sponsor, the site and the IRB, and the site and CRO and/or SMO to demonstrate ongoing communication for the duration of the study? Have all required documentation been forwarded to the IRB, including periodic reports, annual reviews, and study summaries?
Research Charts (Source Documents)	Does the subject's research chart capture sufficient information to demonstrate participation in the clinical trial? Does the information transcribed on the CRFs substantiate the research chart? Are adverse events and serious adverse events recorded in the subject's research chart?

XIII. Clinical Research: Potential Liability

A. Fraud

In clinical research, as in other disciplines, fraud is the deliberate reporting of false or misleading data and/or the withholding of material data, with the intent to mislead the Sponsor, the FDA, or any other party that would have an interest in the data. Once the Sponsor has discovered the fraud, the Sponsor should report the PI's misconduct to the IRB and the FDA for further investigation.

Types of Fraud

The definition of fraud includes:

- ✔ the misrepresentation made by the PI and/or her/his representative by words or through conduct;

- ✔ the misrepresentation made by the PI and/or her/his representative with the knowledge that the representation was not true;

- ✔ representation was made with an intention that should cause the Sponsor to act on it; and

- ✔ the Sponsor's use of the clinical data collected by this PI and/or her/his representative and damage suffered by use of this data.

Who Can Commit Fraud?

Anyone associated with the collection, transcribing, reporting, or monitoring of clinical trial data can commit fraud. This includes the:

- ✔ PI;
- ✔ subinvestigator(s);
- ✔ Clinical Research Study Coordinator;
- ✔ CRA;
- ✔ data manager; and
- ✔ study patient.

Methods Used by the Pharmaceutical Industry to Detect Fraud

These include:

- ✔ identifying the original source data;
- ✔ verifying the existence and accuracy of the source data;

- ✔ challenging the integrity of the data;

- ✔ tracking missing patient records;

- ✔ recognizing fabricated data that will point in the direction of inconclusive results favoring the test article;

- ✔ observing if all the documents are prepared or written by the same person;

- ✔ noting a repeated pattern of data and identifying departures from anticipated trends;

- ✔ determining if the PI and her/his staff have the expertise, capability, and equipment to perform the clinical trial;

- ✔ determining the sequence of events and considering whether or not it was physically possible for the individual(s) to perform the work in the given time frame;

- ✔ observing patient diary cards that are overly pristine;

- ✔ noticing that the handwriting is the same or very similar on the diary cards;

- ✔ observing that the same writing implements were used to complete patient diary cards;

- ✔ observing that the data collected during the course of the clinical trial are too perfect;

- ✔ comparing laboratory data for all subjects enrolled in the clinical trial;

- ✔ observing when patients were seen at the site (e.g., if patients were seen on holidays or weekends when it was not required by the design of the clinical trial);

- ✔ noting a lack of adverse events, especially in certain patient populations with specific disease indications;

- ✔ noting similar blood pressure results for all patients enrolled in the clinical trial; and

- ✔ comparing returned study medication to determine if there is a pattern to the way the blister packs were opened.

Investigator Misconduct

Principal investigator misconduct can be defined as follows:

- ✔ a flagrant, but nondeliberate violation of the Code of Federal Regulations and GCPs;

- ✔ modification of the research data to improve
  - ✔ ability to publish;
  - ✔ accountability;

✔ intentional violation of the code of federal regulations; and

✔ deliberate fabrication of clinical trial results.

B. Negligence

Principal investigator negligence can exist when some of the clinical research data are compromised. The compromised data collected by this PI must be removed from the study database and must not be included in the statistical analysis of the clinical trial.

Principal investigator negligence can result from:

✔ disorganized data and/or

✔ sloppy record keeping.

However, the CRC and the CRA can correct these issues via proper documentation.

Principal investigator negligence can exist when the PI has failed to exercise control over the clinical trial in question. In this instance, all the data generated by this PI is compromised and *all* of the efficacy data collected during the conduct of the clinical trial must be removed from the study database and must not be included in the statistical analysis of the clinical trial.

According to an article in the *New York Times* in May 1999, in an era of managed care the number of private physicians in research since 1990 has almost tripled, and top-enrolling physicians can earn as much as $500,000 to $1 million a year. Pharmaceutical companies and their contractors (CROs/ SMOs) offer large payments to physicians and other allied health professionals to encourage them to enroll patients quickly. There are finder's fees paid to physicians for referring their patients to other physicians conducting clinical trials. In some instances, there are payments to everyone involved in the clinical trial that can assist in the recruitment of patients.

Physicians with substantial compensation at stake may persuade patients to take drugs that are inappropriate or even unsafe for them due to pre-existing medical conditions. Unfortunately, clinical research fraud has become a problem in recent years, resulting in the criminal prosecution of several physicians and study coordinators.

Study patients may also commit fraud by providing false information to participate in a specific study. If patient fraud is detected, notify the Sponsor immediately.

C. Legal Liability and the Clinical Research Coordinator

Criminal Liability is the violation of statutes that carry criminal penalties. These can be state or federal statutes. The Federal FDA regulates clinical research, and a violation of the regulations could result in federal and state criminal prosecution.

Actions that could result in criminal liability include:

- ✔ intentionally creating false or misleading data for submission to the FDA; and
- ✔ assisting with/covering up intentionally false or misleading data created by a PI for the FDA.

In some instances, a criminal prosecutor may go after a CRC to get the CRC to testify against the PI. *A good rule to follow: If a CRC is asked to do something and thinks it is or may be wrong, the CRC should not do it!*

Civil Liability occurs when deliberate actions such as fraud, and nondelinquent actions such as negligence, could result in liability for monetary damages.

A CRC could be considered the agent of the PI if the coordinator performs tasks delegated by the PI. A CRC could also be an agent of their institution (e.g., hospital, medical school, and research institute).

Any actions performed improperly during the course of a clinical trial that result in liability might cause the CRC, the PI, or the institution of employment to be liable.

A PI who does not properly supervise those to whom he/she delegates tasks, resulting in harm to the patient, may also be liable.

There are professionals who think that the one with the most money is the one who is sued. This is not true! The fact that a CRC is not a "deep pocket" will not protect him or her from being named in a lawsuit!

XIV. Writing the Study Summary

A vast amount of information is collected during the course of a controlled clinical study. To transform this raw data into useful information, the Sponsor will subject the data to rigorous analyses. The following are typical of the analyses and presentations prepared by the Sponsor.

A. Biostatistical Report

Following the statistical analysis of the data collected during the study, comprehensive computer-generated tabulations are prepared to summarize the trends and changes that occurred. An interpretation of these statistical results is provided in the biostatistical report, which is typically written by a biostatistician.

B. Integrated Clinical Study Report

To present the results of the study to the FDA and other regulatory agencies around the world, the Sponsor will prepare a report that provides a detailed description of the methods, results, and conclusions drawn from the study. This report integrates the key aspects of the biostatistical report with clinical interpretations of the study results. In this manner, a comprehensive overview of the study is prepared for future reference.

C. Articles for Publication

The results of key studies are often written up for submission to scientific journals. The PI or sub-investigators may be given the opportunity to draft the manuscript based on data contained in the Integrated Clinical Study Report. The Sponsor may offer technical or editorial assistance in preparing these articles. Alternately, data from a study may be presented as an abstract or poster at a scientific meeting.

XV. Achieving Credibility and Recognition as a Clinical Research Coordinator

Achieving credibility and recognition as a CRC in the pharmaceutical industry is not an easy undertaking. To be successful in the pharmaceutical research industry, it is essential to be seen as competent, believable, and confident by the CRAs, Sponsors, and others.

Three important ways to enhance your credibility as a research professional are to continually radiate a professional image, to demonstrate your integrity, and to build good professional relationships.

Presenting a professional relationship utilizing written correspondence can be achieved in many ways.

> ✔ Follow a business letter format.

> ✔ Use letterhead and include the name of the study about which you are writing.

> ✔ Do not write personal comments or opinions in study-related correspondence.

> ✔ Remember that people you have never met may review anything you write. It may become a permanent part of a study's regulatory file.

> ✔ Use spell-check, and remember to proofread everything to ensure you are using the correct words (i.e., "principal" investigator versus "principle" investigator).

> ✔ Save personal comments for a time when you are speaking person-to-person.

Presenting a professional image utilizing voice mail can also be achieved.

> ✔ Generally, the same rules apply to voice and written correspondence.

> ✔ Remember that voice-messaging systems can be an open forum, as your message can be forwarded to multiple people.

> ✔ Take a moment and make sure you are leaving a message for the correct person at his/her extension. If you inadvertently leave a voice mail message on the wrong extension, the message may take on a "life of its own," as it is forwarded companywide until/if the message reaches the person for whom it was intended.

> ✔ Messages should be *short* and to the point.

> ✔ Briefly indicate the reason why you are calling. This will better enable the CRA to quickly respond to your needs.

Presenting a professional image utilizing e-mail can be achieved in many ways.

- ✔ E-mail messaging can be an open forum because your message, even if it is bcc (blind carbon copied) and marked "confidential," can be forwarded to multiple people.

- ✔ Make sure you are sending the e-mail to the correct e-mail address.

- ✔ Do not forward the following types of e-mail messages:
  - ✔ chain e-mails; and
  - ✔ e-mails using profanity or anything not related to the study.

- ✔ Do not put your favorite CRA on any kind of e-mail mailing list. Sponsors may periodically monitor their employees' e-mail messages.

Demonstrating your integrity can be achieved via the following ways:

- ✔ Making sure you keep commitments.

- ✔ Letting the CRA know if you are not going to be ready for his/her visit, not at the last minute, but in enough time so that the visit can be rescheduled.

- ✔ Knowing that mistakes are made by everyone and that research is a team effort (the CRA is only doing his/her job).

- ✔ Not taking on more work than you can realistically handle.

- ✔ Being careful not to speak negatively about another professional. You never know when someone who knows of the individual about whom you are speaking may be listening and repeat the conversation.

XVI. Appendices

APPENDIX I: Helpful Sources

A. Names and Addresses of Clinical Research Resources

Membership Organizations

DIA (Drug Information Association)
800 Enterprise Road
Suite 200
Horsham, PA 19044-3595
Telephone: 215-442-6100
Fax: 215-442-6199
E-mail: dia@diahome.org

American Society of Law, Medicine and Ethics
765 Commonwealth Avenue
Suite #1634
Boston, MA 02215
Telephone :   617-262-4990
Fax: 617-437-7596
Web address: http://www.aslme.org

PRIM&R (Public Responsibility in Medicine and Research)
126 Brookline Avenue
Suite 202
Boston, MA 02215-3920
Telephone: 617-423-4112
Fax: 617-423-1185
Web address: http://www.primr.org
PRIM&R's Executive Office is also the Administrative Site for ARENA
(Applied Research Ethics National Association)

ACRP (Association of Clinical Research Professionals)
500 Montgomery Street
Suite 800
Alexandria, VA 22314
Telephone: 703-254-8100
Fax: 703-254-8101
E-mail: office@acrpnet.org

Coordinator Resources

MedTrials, Inc.
2777 Stemmons Freeway
Suite #900
Dallas, TX 75207
Telephone: 214-630-0288
Fax: 214-630-0289
Web address: http://www.medtrials.com
Develops site efficiency tools to increase productivity and optimize performance and regulatory compliance. They offer a line of performance products for investigative sites including:
> *Correspondence templates*
> *Source document templates*
> *Subject identification stickers*
> *Visit reminder cards*
> *Study day estimators*
> *Reference charts*
> *Patient and research staff educational materials*
> *Standard operating procedure templates for clinical research sites*

Publications

Ethics and Regulations of Clinical Research by Robert J. Levine
2nd Edition 1988—Paperback $25.00
Yale University Press—203-432-0960

Glossary of Lay Language Synonyms for Common Terms Used in Informed Consent Documents for Clinical Studies—A Handbook for Clinical Researchers by Deborrah Norris
1996—Paperback $39.95
Plexus Publishing, Inc.—609-654-6500

Seminars/Workshops

Contact the following organizations directly for information:

South Florida Coordinating Services (training specific to CRCs)
Telephone: 954-254-6636

WIRB (Western Institutional Review Board)
Telephone: 360-754-9248 *(for their one-day coordinator class)*
                 360-943-1410
E-mail: wirb@wirb.com

DIA (Drug Information Association)
Telephone: 215-628-2288

MED EXEC International
Telephone: 800-507-5277

PRIM&R/ARENA
Telephone: 617-423-4112

American Society of Law, Medicine and Ethics
Telephone: 617-262-4990

FDA (Food and Drug Administration)
Telephone: 301-443-2894

Chesapeake Research Review, Inc.
Matthew Whalen, Ph.D.
President, Chesapeake Research Review, Inc.
9130 Guilford Road
Columbia, MD 21046
Telephone: 410-884-2900

KDO Consulting, LLC
Pharmaceutical Clinical Trials
Monitoring and Auditing
213 Barton Ave.
Pt. Pleasant, NJ 08742
Telephone: 732-701-0893
Fax: 732-782-0255
E-mail: kyle739@comcast.net

ACRP (Association of Clinical Research Professionals)
Telephone: 202-737-8100

Enterprise Research Services, Inc.
3915 SW Harbor Drive
Lee's Summit, MO 64082-4632
Telephone: 816-537-4222
Fax: 816-537-9746

Legal Services

Francis X. Sexton, Jr., Esq.
44 W. Flagler Street
Suite 2450
Miami, FL 33130
Telephone: 305-371-2756
Fax: 305-372-2744
E-mail: fsexton@silveriohall.com

Commercial IRBs (Central IRBs)

(For a complete listing of all commercial IRBs, contact HIMA)

Health Industry Manufacturers Association (HIMA)

1200 G Street NW

Suite #400

Washington, DC 20005-3814

Telephone: 202-783-8700

Fax: 202-783-8750

Web address: http://www.himanet.com

Employment Services

MED EXEC International

100 North Brand Blvd.

Suite #306-308

Glendale, CA 91203

Telephone: 818-552-2036; (toll-free) 800-507-5277

Web address: http://www.medexecintl.com

Contact: Rosemary Christopher

(Placement Services for CRCs; Site Managers; Site Directors; Patient Recruitment Specialists)

NIH Certification

(Noted certification provided at no cost; Web-based instructional courses)

E-mail: http://www.cancer.gov/clinicaltrials/resources

CRC Certification

(Contact them directly for additional information)

ACRP (Association of Clinical Research Professionals)

Telephone: 202-737-8100

B. Important FDA Contacts for IRBs and Clinical Investigators

GENERAL QUESTIONS

- Call 301-827-1685 (Health Assessment Policy Staff, Office of Health Affairs, Office of the Commissioner) for:

    Questions about or suggestions for these Information Sheets

    General questions about FDA human subject protection regulations [21 CFR parts 50 and 56]

    Reports made pursuant to 21 CFR 56.108(b) and 56.113 including:

    —unanticipated problems involving risks to subjects 21 CFR 56.108(b)(1);

  —serious or continuing noncompliance (by an investigator) with FDA regulations or with the IRB's determinations 21 CFR 56.108(b)(2); or

  —suspension or termination of IRB approval of a protocol 21 CFR 56.108(b)(3).

- Call 800-993-0098 or 301-827-3156 (Automatic Fax-on-Demand line) for:

  Copies of the FDA human subject protection regulations [21 CFR parts 50 and 56] and general interpretive documents (e.g., individual FDA Information Sheets).

- The FDA Information Sheets for Instructional Review Boards and Clinical Investigators are available on the FDA Home Page http://www.fda.gov/oc/oha/IRB/toc.html

- CBER new document list e-mail subscription: Send an e-mail message: "SUBSCRIBE CBERINFO youremailaddress@yourdomain" to: "FDAlists@www.fda.gov"

- CBER bounce-back e-mail document list: Send a blank e-mail message to: "doc_list@al.cber.fda.gov"

DEVICE QUESTIONS—Center for Device Evaluation and Radiologic Health (CDRH)

- Call 800-638-2041 (Division of Small Manufacturers Assistance, CDRH) for copies of publications pertaining to device studies.

- Call 301-594-1190 (Program Operation Staff, CDRH) for questions about:

  •Whether an investigational device exemption (IDE) is required for a device study

  •Whether a device study is deemed "significant risk" or "nonsignificant risk"

  •Whether a device is approved for marketing

- Call 301-594-4718 (Bioresearch Monitoring Branch, Office of Compliance, CDRH) for questions about:

  •Human subject protection regulations pertaining to devices [21 CFR parts 50, 56, 812, 813, and 814]

• CDRH-assigned IRB Inspections (e.g., "483s" and "Warning Letters")
CDRH-assigned Clinical Investigator Inspections (e.g., "483s" and "Warning Letters")

• CDRH-assigned Sponsor Inspections (e.g., "483s" and "Warning Letters")

• "Device Advice" on the Web: http://www.fda.gov/cdrh/devadvice

OTHER

• Call (modem) 800-222-0185 (FDA computer Bulletin Board) for: [login name= "BBS"]

• FDA Federal Register notices, new releases, product approval lists, and selected consumer articles.

• Call 301-496-7041 (Office for Protection from Research Risks-OPRR) for:

• Guidance about "Assurances" with the Department of Health and Human Services (HHS)

• questions regarding 45 CFR part 46

World Wide Web Sites of Interest for Human Subject Protection Information

FDA Home Page: http://www.fda.gov
(714) 798-7769

This is the gateway to all FDA information, with sections for the product-specific centers (Drugs, Biologics, Medical Devices, Veterinary Drugs, Foods, Toxicological Research) and FDA-wide subjects.

MINNEAPOLIS District
240 Hennepin Avenue
Minneapolis, Minnesota 55401-1912   Minnesota, Wisconsin, North Dakota,
(612) 334-4100 EXT 162   South Dakota

NASHVILLE District
297 Plus Park Boulevard
Nashville, Tennessee 37217   Alabama, Tennesse
(615) 781-5378

NEW JERSEY District
Waterview Corp. Center
10 Waterway Bend, 3rd Floor
Parsippany, New Jersey 07054   New Jersey
(201) 526-6000

NEW ORLEANS District
4298 Elysian Fields Avenue
New Orleans, Louisiana 70122   Louisiana, Mississippi
(504) 589-6344

NEW YORK District
850 Third Avenue
Brooklyn, New York 11232-1593   New York City, Long Island
(718) 340-7000

PHILADELPHIA District
2nd and Chestnut Streets
Room 900
Philadelphia, Pennsylvania 19106   Delaware, Pennsylvania
(215) 597-4390

SEATTLE District
22201 23rd Drive S.E.
P.O. Box 3012
Bothell, Washington 98041-3012   Alaska, Idaho, Oregon, Montana, Washington
(206) 483-4941

SAN FRANCISCO District
1431 Harbor Bay Parkway
Alameda, California 94502-7070   California (northern), Hawaii, Nevada,
(510) 337-6733   American Samoa, Guam, Pacific Trust Territory

SAN JUAN District
#466 Fernandez Juncos Avenue
Stop 8 1/2
San Juan, Puerto Rico 00901-3223   Puerto Rico
(809) 729-6608

Information for Health Professionals: http://www.fda.gov/oc/oha
This provides information targeted to this specific group.

Information Sheets: http://www.fda.gov/oc/oha/IRB/toc.html

This is the FDA Information Sheets for Institutional Review Boards and Clinical Investigators.

FDA Disqualified Investigator List: http://www.fda.gov/oc/oha/list2.htm

This is a cumulative list of clinical investigators who have been, or are currently, disqualified from access to investigational products, or had their use of investigational products restricted.

PHS List of Investigators Subject
to Administrative Action: http://silk.nih.gov/public/cbz1bje@www.
orilist.html

This list includes the investigators disqualified by FDA, but also those subject to action by the HHS Office of Research Integrity.

Government Printing Office (Federal
Register, Code of Federal Regulations,
Congressional Record): http://www.access.gpo.gov/su_docs
(This is the site for any Federal Register document since 1994, and any section in the entire Code of Federal Regulations.)

Information for Health
Professionals: http://www.fda.gov/oc/oha

FDA Disqualified Investigator List: http://www.fda.gov/oc/oha/list2.htm

FDA Debarred Persons List http://www.fda.gov/ora/compliance_ref/debar/
default.htm

PHS List of Investigators Subject
to Administrative Action: http://silk.nih.gov/public/cbz1bje.@www.
orilist.html

Government Printing Office
(Federal Register, Code of Federal
Regulations, Congressional Record): http://www.access.gpo.gov/su_docs

Medwatch http://www.fda.gov/medwatch

Freedom of Information Act (FOIA) http://www.fda.gov/foi

FDA Dockets	http://www.fda.gov/ohrms/dockets.htm
Laws enforced by FDA	http://www.fda.gov/opacom/laws/lawtoc.htm
FD&C Act	http://www.fda.gov/opacom/laws/fdcact/fdctoc.htm
FDA Modernization Act of 1997	http://www.fda.gov/cder/guidance/105-115.htm
CDRH-Guidance CDER-Related Documents	http://www.fda.gov/cdrh/modact.modguid.html www.fda.gov/cder/fdama/default.htm (scroll to Modernization)
Expedited Safety Reporting Requirements Oct 7, 1997 Federal Register Final rule	http://www.fda.gov/cder/regguide.htm click on: (federal register-GPO)(Federal register)(1997) (final rules & regulations) enter date: (on 10/07/97) search terms: (expedited)
Pediatric Medicine Page	http://www.fda.gov/cder/pediatric
CDER organizational chart	http://www.fda.gov/cder/cderorg.htm
CDER alphab employee directory	http://www.fda.gov/cder/directoruies/cderdir.txt
CDRH organization structure	http://www.fda.gov/cdrh/organiz.html
CDRH Device Advice	http://www.fda.gov/cdrh/devadvice
Drug approvals list	http://www.fda.gov/cder/da/da.htm
New drug approval packages	http://www.fda.gov/cder/foi/nda/index.htm
Orange book (Approved Drugs)	http://www.fda.gov/cder/orange/adp.htm
Computerized systems used in clincial trials	http://www.fda.gov/cder/guidance/indext.htm (compliance (draft))
Archiving submissions in electronic format	http://www.fda.gov/cder/guidance.arcguide.pdf
Accepting electronic CRF	http://www.fda.gov/cder/mapp/6010-1.pdf
List of available guidance documents	http://www.fda.gov/cder/guidance/index.htm
Warning letters	http://www.fda.gov/foi/warning.htm

National Drug Code (NDC) directory	http://www.fda.gov/cder/ndc/index.htm
Pharmacy Compounding	http://www.fda.gov/cder/news/pharmcomm.htm
Bioresearch Monitoring Information Systems File: clinical investigators, CROs and IRBs from FDA 1571 & 1572s	http://www.fda.gov/cder/foi/special/bmis/index.htm
IDE Policies and Procedures	http://www.fda.gov/cdrh/ode/idepolcy.pdf
OPRR	http://www.nih.gov/grants/oprr/oprr.htm
OPRR IRB Guidebook	http://www.nih.gov/grants/oprr/irb/irb_guidebook.htm
OPRR IRB MPA list	http://www.nih.gov/grants/oprr/mpalist.htm
HHS Employee and Organizational Dir	http://ds1.psc.dhhs.gov/hhsdir/eeQ.stm
National Bioethics Advisory Comm.	http://bioethics.gov/cgi-bin/bioeth_counter.pl
ICH	http://www.fda.gov/cder/guidance/index.htm (then scroll down)

APPENDIX II: Forms Used During the Course of a Clinical Study

Form 1. INFORMATION REGARDING PARTICIPATION IN A CLINICAL TRIAL

What Is a Clinical Trial?

A clinical trial is a research study conducted to evaluate the safety and effectiveness of a new medication or a medical device not yet available to the public. A clinical trial must adhere to the strict regulatory guidelines established by the Food and Drug Administration (FDA). *Participation in a clinical trial is voluntary.* Your physician may suggest benefits from participating in a clinical trial; however, the decision is yours alone to make.

Most clinical trials are conducted in phases. There are four main phases of clinical trials:
> Phase I
> Phase II
> Phase III
> Phase IV

Phase I clinical trials help to establish the safest dose of a medication and procedure guidelines as well as the safety profile of the new medication or medical device. These clinical trials are generally conducted in a small number of healthy volunteers with no critical medical conditions.

Phase II clinical trials help to establish the doses determined in the Phase I study are safe and effective. These clinical trials are generally conducted in a larger number of volunteers with the medical condition the drug or device is being developed to treat.

Phase III clinical trials help to confirm the doses and side effects of the new medication or medical device. Volunteers for this phase of a clinical trial can range from 100–5,000 and may be conducted worldwide.

Phase IV clinical trials are generally performed after the drug or medical device has been approved by the FDA and further helps to evaluate the effectiveness of the drug or medical device.

Why Do People Volunteer to Participate in a Clinical Trial?

People volunteer to participate in a clinical trial for various reasons:
> ✔ To receive the latest, most advanced medications long before the medication has been made available to the general public
>
> ✔ To have a medical option to their current medical treatment which may not be effective
>
> ✔ To assist in the development of a new medication or device to assist others with a similar condition

What can you expect if you volunteer to participate in a Clinical Trial?

- ✔ A full medical evaluation and diagnosis is made by a qualified physician

- ✔ Close medical monitoring, including study related laboratory tests, x-rays, etc., often at no cost to you

- ✔ Full disclosure of the risks and benefits associated with your participation in the clinical trial

- ✔ Regular medical examinations to evaluate your progress

Your participation in a clinical trial begins after you have been given an informed consent, which has been approved by an Independent Institutional Review Board (IRB), whose purpose is mainly the protection of human volunteers. *When all your questions and concerns have been addressed by the physician in charge of the clinical trial and the informed consent has been signed and documented, the clinical trial may begin. Remember—no study-related procedures can be performed until after you have signed the informed consent document.*

Participation in a clinical trial is voluntary—you may withdraw your consent at any time during the conduct of the study without any negative effects related to your medical care.

How Does This Affect Care Received From Your Primary Care Physician?

Your participation in a clinical trial will not affect the care you are receiving from your primary care physician. You are encouraged to talk to your doctor about your participation in a clinical trial. The physician conducting the clinical trial does not replace your physician but works with the physician to provide you with additional healthcare options. Your records during your participation in a clinical trial may be shared with your physician, or they may remain confidential at your request.

Participation in a clinical trial is a commitment between you and the physician conducting the clinical trial. It is important for your own safety and well-being you follow the clinical trial instructions and you keep all appointments required by the clinical trial and to take the study medication or use the medical device as instructed.

It may be helpful to know your participation in a clinical trial may assist in the development of a new medication or medical device, which could benefit many people suffering from the same medical condition.

Form 2. THE STATEMENT OF INVESTIGATOR FORM (FDA 1572)

DEPARTMENT OF HEALTH AND HUMAN SERVICES PUBLIC HEALTH SERVICE FOOD AND DRUG ADMINISTRATION **STATEMENT OF INVESTIGATOR** *(TITLE 21, CODE OF FEDERAL REGULATIONS (CFR) PART 312)* (See instructions on reverse side.)	Form Approved: OMB No. 0910-0014. Expiration Date: January 31, 2006. *See OMB Statement on Reverse.*
	NOTE: No investigator may participate in an investigation until he/she provides the sponsor with a completed, signed Statement of Investigator, Form FDA 1572 (21 CFR 312.53(c)).

1. NAME AND ADDRESS OF INVESTIGATOR

2. EDUCATION, TRAINING, AND EXPERIENCE THAT QUALIFIES THE INVESTIGATOR AS AN EXPERT IN THE CLINICAL INVESTIGATION OF THE DRUG FOR THE USE UNDER INVESTIGATION. ONE OF THE FOLLOWING IS ATTACHED.

☐ CURRICULUM VITAE   ☐ OTHER STATEMENT OF QUALIFICATIONS

3. NAME AND ADDRESS OF ANY MEDICAL SCHOOL, HOSPITAL OR OTHER RESEARCH FACILITY WHERE THE CLINICAL INVESTIGATION(S) WILL BE CONDUCTED.

4. NAME AND ADDRESS OF ANY CLINICAL LABORATORY FACILITIES TO BE USED IN THE STUDY.

5. NAME AND ADDRESS OF THE INSTITUTIONAL REVIEW BOARD (IRB) THAT IS RESPONSIBLE FOR REVIEW AND APPROVAL OF THE STUDY(IES).

6. NAMES OF THE SUBINVESTIGATORS *(e.g., research fellows, residents, associates)* **WHO WILL BE ASSISTING THE INVESTIGATOR IN THE CONDUCT OF THE INVESTIGATION(S).**

7. NAME AND CODE NUMBER, IF ANY, OF THE PROTOCOL(S) IN THE IND FOR THE STUDY(IES) TO BE CONDUCTED BY THE INVESTIGATOR.

FORM FDA 1572 (1/03)   PREVIOUS EDITION IS OBSOLETE.   PAGE 1 OF 2

8. ATTACH THE FOLLOWING CLINICAL PROTOCOL INFORMATION:

☐ FOR PHASE 1 INVESTIGATIONS, A GENERAL OUTLINE OF THE PLANNED INVESTIGATION INCLUDING THE ESTIMATED DURATION OF THE STUDY AND THE MAXIMUM NUMBER OF SUBJECTS THAT WILL BE INVOLVED.

☐ FOR PHASE 2 OR 3 INVESTIGATIONS, AN OUTLINE OF THE STUDY PROTOCOL INCLUDING AN APPROXIMATION OF THE NUMBER OF SUBJECTS TO BE TREATED WITH THE DRUG AND THE NUMBER TO BE EMPLOYED AS CONTROLS, IF ANY; THE CLINICAL USES TO BE INVESTIGATED; CHARACTERISTICS OF SUBJECTS BY AGE, SEX, AND CONDITION; THE KIND OF CLINICAL OBSERVATIONS AND LABORATORY TESTS TO BE CONDUCTED; THE ESTIMATED DURATION OF THE STUDY; AND COPIES OR A DESCRIPTION OF CASE REPORT FORMS TO BE USED.

9. COMMITMENTS:

I agree to conduct the study(ies) in accordance with the relevant, current protocol(s) and will only make changes in a protocol after notifying the sponsor, except when necessary to protect the safety, rights, or welfare of subjects.

I agree to personally conduct or supervise the described investigation(s).

I agree to inform any patients, or any persons used as controls, that the drugs are being used for investigational purposes and I will ensure that the requirements relating to obtaining informed consent in 21 CFR Part 50 and institutional review board (IRB) review and approval in 21 CFR Part 56 are met.

I agree to report to the sponsor adverse experiences that occur in the course of the investigation(s) in accordance with 21 CFR 312.64.

I have read and understand the information in the investigator's brochure, including the potential risks and side effects of the drug.

I agree to ensure that all associates, colleagues, and employees assisting in the conduct of the study(ies) are informed about their obligations in meeting the above commitments.

I agree to maintain adequate and accurate records in accordance with 21 CFR 312.62 and to make those records available for inspection in accordance with 21 CFR 312.68.

I will ensure that an IRB that complies with the requirements of 21 CFR Part 56 will be responsible for the initial and continuing review and approval of the clinical investigation. I also agree to promptly report to the IRB all changes in the research activity and all unanticipated problems involving risks to human subjects or others. Additionally, I will not make any changes in the research without IRB approval, except where necessary to eliminate apparent immediate hazards to human subjects.

I agree to comply with all other requirements regarding the obligations of clinical investigators and all other pertinent requirements in 21 CFR Part 312.

INSTRUCTIONS FOR COMPLETING FORM FDA 1572
STATEMENT OF INVESTIGATOR:

1. Complete all sections. Attach a separate page if additional space is needed.

2. Attach curriculum vitae or other statement of qualifications as described in Section 2.

3. Attach protocol outline as described in Section 8.

4. Sign and date below.

5. FORWARD THE COMPLETED FORM AND ATTACHMENTS TO THE SPONSOR. The sponsor will incorporate this information along with other technical data into an Investigational New Drug Application (IND).

10. SIGNATURE OF INVESTIGATOR	11. DATE

(**WARNING:** A willfully false statement is a criminal offense. U.S.C. Title 18, Sec. 1001.)

Public reporting burden for this collection of information is estimated to average 100 hours per response, including the time for reviewing instructions, searching existing data sources, gathering and maintaining the data needed, and completing reviewing the collection of information. Send comments regarding this burden estimate or any other aspect of this collection of information, including suggestions for reducing this burden to:

Food and Drug Administration
CBER (HFM-99)
1401 Rockville Pike
Rockville, MD 20852-1448

Food and Drug Administration
CDER (HFD-94)
12229 Wilkins Avenue
Rockville, MD 20852

"An agency may not conduct or sponsor, and a person is not required to respond to, a collection of information unless it displays a currently valid OMB control number."

Please **DO NOT RETURN** this application to this address.

Example of Form 2, FDA 1572, Completed

DEPARTMENT OF HEALTH AND HUMAN SERVICES PUBLIC HEALTH SERVICE FOOD AND DRUG ADMINISTRATION **STATEMENT OF INVESTIGATOR** *(TITLE 21, CODE OF FEDERAL REGULATIONS (CFR) PART 312)* (See instructions on reverse side.)	Form Approved: OMB No. 0910-0014. Expiration Date: January 31, 2006. *See OMB Statement on Reverse.*
	NOTE: No investigator may participate in an investigation until he/she provides the sponsor with a completed, signed Statement of Investigator, Form FDA 1572 (21 CFR 312.53(c)).

1. NAME AND ADDRESS OF INVESTIGATOR

Include the facility address where the physician is affiliated.
Include any co-PIs (rare).
A separate 1572 needs to be completed for each PI.

2. EDUCATION, TRAINING, AND EXPERIENCE THAT QUALIFIES THE INVESTIGATOR AS AN EXPERT IN THE CLINICAL INVESTIGATION OF THE DRUG FOR THE USE UNDER INVESTIGATION. ONE OF THE FOLLOWING IS ATTACHED.

☒ CURRICULUM VITAE   ☐ OTHER STATEMENT OF QUALIFICATIONS

3. NAME AND ADDRESS OF ANY MEDICAL SCHOOL, HOSPITAL OR OTHER RESEARCH FACILITY WHERE THE CLINICAL INVESTIGATION(S) WILL BE CONDUCTED.

Important: List the names and addresses of any facility that will be evaluating or performing tests on a subject.

EXAMPLE →

ABC Research Centers of America
1234 South Park Road
Anytown, USA

ABC Research Centers of America
4455 West 50th Avenue
Anytown, USA

Rehab Associates
4234 West 50th Avenue
Anytown, USA

4. NAME AND ADDRESS OF ANY CLINICAL LABORATORY FACILITIES TO BE USED IN THE STUDY.

Important: List the names and addresses of each laboratory processing laboratory samples including a local lab, if applicable, when using a central lab. Include the name and address of any facility reviewing ECGs and CT scans, if applicable.

Central Research Laboratories
1254 South Park Road
Anytown, USA

Radiology Associates
5425 SE 5th Avenue
Irvine, California

5. NAME AND ADDRESS OF THE INSTITUTIONAL REVIEW BOARD (IRB) THAT IS RESPONSIBLE FOR REVIEW AND APPROVAL OF THE STUDY(IES).

Institutional Review of Anytown
4455 South 8th Street
Anytown, USA

If the sponsor has contracted with a central IRB, you are not obligated to use the central IRB if you have a local IRB. Check with the local IRB to see if their schedule will accommodate the sponsor's timelines.

6. NAMES OF THE SUBINVESTIGATORS *(e.g., research fellows, residents, associates)* **WHO WILL BE ASSISTING THE INVESTIGATOR IN THE CONDUCT OF THE INVESTIGATION(S).**

List all subinvestigators in this section. Check with the sponsor to see if the names of additional research staff need to be included, i.e., CRC, pharmacist.

Allan Jones, MD
John Allen, MD
Alex Campbell, MD
Marc Ackerman, DO
Sally Chapps, RN, CRC
Michael Sams, Phar. D.

7. NAME AND CODE NUMBER, IF ANY, OF THE PROTOCOL(S) IN THE IND FOR THE STUDY(IES) TO BE CONDUCTED BY THE INVESTIGATOR.

Make sure you list the complete title of the protocol, include the IND# if available.

Note: If the sponsor provides the Form FDA 1572 on a computer disk, make sure you make the form print out as ONE page, not two.

FORM FDA 1572 (1/03)   PREVIOUS EDITION IS OBSOLETE.   PAGE 1 OF 2

8. ATTACH THE FOLLOWING CLINICAL PROTOCOL INFORMATION:

[X] FOR PHASE 1 INVESTIGATIONS, A GENERAL OUTLINE OF THE PLANNED INVESTIGATION INCLUDING THE ESTIMATED DURATION OF THE STUDY AND THE MAXIMUM NUMBER OF SUBJECTS THAT WILL BE INVOLVED.

[ ] FOR PHASE 2 OR 3 INVESTIGATIONS, AN OUTLINE OF THE STUDY PROTOCOL INCLUDING AND APPROXIMATION OF THE NUMBER OF SUBJECTS TO BE TREATED WITH THE DRUG AND THE NUMBER TO BE EMPLOYED AS CONTROLS, IF ANY; THE CLINICAL USES TO BE INVESTIGATED; CHARACTERISTICS OF SUBJECTS BY AGE, SEX, AND CONDITION; THE KIND OF CLINICAL OBSERVATIONS AND LABORATORY TESTS TO BE CONDUCTED; THE ESTIMATED DURATION OF THE STUDY; AND COPIES OR A DESCRIPTION OF CASE REPORT FORMS TO BE USED.

9. COMMITMENTS

I agree to conduct the study(ies) in accordance with the relevant, current protocol(s) and will only make changes in a protocol after notifying the sponsor, except when necessary to protect the safety, rights, or welfare of subjects.

I agree to personally conduct or supervise the described investigation(s).

I agree to inform any patients, or any persons used as controls, that the drugs are being used for investigational purposes and I will ensure that the requirements relating to obtaining informed consent in 21 CFR Part 50 and institutional review board (IRB) review and approval in 21 CFR Part 56 are met.

I agree to report to the sponsor adverse experiences that occur in the course of the investigation(s) in accordance with 21 CFR 312.64.

I have read and understand the information in the investigator's brochure, including the potential risks and side effects of the drug.

I agree to ensure that all associates, colleagues, and employees assisting in the conduct of the study(ies) are informed about their obligations in meeting the above commitments.

I agree to maintain adequate and accurate records in accordance with 21 CFR 312.62 and to make those records available for inspections in accordance with 21 CFR 312.68.

I will ensure that an IRB that complies with the requirements of 21 CFR Part 56 will be responsible for the initial and continuing review and approval of the clinical investigation. I also agree to promptly report to the IRB all changes in the research activity and all unanticipated problems involving risks to human subjects or others. Additionally, I will not make any changes in the research without IRB approval, except where necessary to eliminate apparent immediate hazards to human subjects.

I agree to comply with all other requirements regarding the obligations of clinical investigations and all other pertinent requirements in 21 CFR Part 312.

INSTRUCTIONS FOR COMPLETING FORM FDA 1572
STATEMENT OF INVESTIGATOR:

1. Complete all sections. Attach a separate page if addtional space is needed.

2. Attach curriculum vitae or other statement of qualifications as described in Section 2.

3. Attach protocol outline as described in Section 8.

4. Sign and date below.

5. FORWARD THE COMPLETED FORM AND ATTACHMENTS TO THE SPONSOR. The sponsor will incorporate this information along with other technical data into an Investigational New Drug Application (IND).

10. SIGNATURE OF INVESTIGATOR	11. DATE
John R. Smith	2/2/05

(**WARNING**: A wilfully false statement is a criminal offense. U. S. C. Title 18, Sec. 1001.)

Public reporting burden for this collection of information is estimated to average 100 hours per response, including the time for reviewing instructions, searching existing data sources, gathering and maintaining the data needed, and completing reviewing the collection of information. Send comments regarding this burden estimate or any other aspect of this collection of information, including suggestions for reducing this burden to:

Food and Drug Administration
CBER (HFM-99)
1401 Rockville Pike
Rockville, MD 20852-1448

Food and Drug Administration
CDER (HFD-94)
12229 Wilkins Avenue
Rockville, MD 20852

"An agency may not conduct or sponsor, and a person is not required to respond to, a collection of information unless it displays a currently valid OMB control number."

Please **DO NOT RETURN** this application to this address.

Form 3. THE ADMINISTRATIVE CHECKLIST

Protocol # _____

Protocol Title _____

_____

Sponsor _____

Test Article _____

Clinical Research Associate _____

Phone # _____ Fax # _____

E-mail Address _____

Name of Laboratory _____

Phone # _____ Fax # _____

Institutional Review Board (IRB) _____

Chairperson _____

Phone # _____ Fax # _____

E-mail Address _____

Protocol Approval Date _____ Informed Consent Date _____

Principal Investigator _____

Subinvestigator(s) _____

_____

Study Coordinator _____

Study Initiation Date _____ Investigator Meeting Date _____

Documents on File

__ Form FDA 1572	__ Completed Financial Disclosure Form
__ CVs/Medical License	__ Serious Adverse Event Form
__ Laboratory Certification	__ Laboratory Normals/Values
__ Complete Signed Protocol	__ MedWatch Forms
__ Protocol Signature Page	__ Site Signature Log
__ Protocol Amendments	__ Laboratory Submission Reports
__ IRB Membership List	__ Monitor Site Visit Log
__ IRB Approval Letter	__ Informed Consent Approval Letter
__ IRB Approved Informed Consents	__ Telephone Log
__ Original Signed Consents	__ Letter of Indemnification
__ Investigator Brochure	__ Shipping Invoices for ALL Supplies
__ Drug Accountability	__ On-going Correspondence
__ Enrollment Logs	__ Informed Consent Logs
__ Investigator Meeting Agenda	__ Investigator/Meeting Attendee List
__ Confidentiality Agreement	__ Delegation of Responsibility
__ Miscellaneous Sponsor Forms	__ Other Source Documents

NOTE:

All financial records including the following *SHOULD NOT* be part of the Site Binder and should be kept separate:

✔ study budget;

✔ signed Study Agreement with financial compensation; and

✔ signed Financial Disclosure Form (may be included depending upon Sponsor's SOPs).

However, these can be requested by the FDA during an audit.

Form 4. INITIAL ADVERSE EXPERIENCE REPORT SHEET

Date _____

Study Protocol # _____

Study Investigator _____

Subject I.D. (initials and #) _____

Date subject entered study _____

If subject discontinued study:

Date drug discontinued _____

Date subject discontinued study _____

Description of adverse experience _____

_____

*Diagnostic procedure(s) performed _____

_____

Relationship to study drug ("not related," "possibly," "probably," "definitely") _____

Subject's present condition _____

Was subject hospitalized? _____

Was sponsor notified? _____

Name of sponsor's representative contacted/date contacted _____

May not be applicable

_____
Clinical Research Coordinator (*signature*)

Form 5. THE MEDWATCH ADVERSE EXPERIENCE FORM

MEDWATCH

THE FDA MEDICAL PRODUCTS REPORTING PROGRAM

For **VOLUNTARY** reporting
by health professionals of adverse
events and product problems

Page ____ of ____

Form Approved: OMB No. 0910-0291 Expires:12/31/94
See OMB statement on reverse

FDA Use Only

Triage unit
sequence #

A. Patient information

1. Patient identifier	2. Age at time of event: ____ or Date of birth: ____	3. Sex ☐ female ☐ male	4. Weight ____ lbs or ____ kgs

In confidence

B. Adverse event or product problem

1. ☐ **Adverse event** and/or ☐ **Product problem** (e.g., defects/malfunctions)

2. **Outcomes attributed to adverse event** (check all that apply)
- ☐ death ____ (mo/day/yr)
- ☐ life-threatening
- ☐ hospitalization – initial or prolonged
- ☐ disability
- ☐ congenital anomaly
- ☐ required intervention to prevent permanent impairment/damage
- ☐ other: ____

3. **Date of event** (mo/day/yr)

4. **Date of this report** (mo/day/yr)

5. **Describe event or problem**

6. **Relevant tests/laboratory data,** including dates

7. **Other relevant history, including preexisting medical conditions** (e.g., allergies, race, pregnancy, smoking and alcohol use, hepatic/renal dysfunction, etc.)

C. Suspect medication(s)

1. **Name** (give labeled strength & mfr/labeler, if known)

#1

#2

2. **Dose, frequency & route used**	3. **Therapy dates** (if unknown, give duration) from/to (or best estimate)
#1	#1
#2	#2

4. **Diagnosis for use** (indication)

#1

#2

5. **Event abated after use stopped or dose reduced**
- #1 ☐ yes ☐ no ☐ doesn't apply
- #2 ☐ yes ☐ no ☐ doesn't apply

6. **Lot #** (if known)	7. **Exp. date** (if known)
#1	#1
#2	#2

8. **Event reappeared after reintroduction**
- #1 ☐ yes ☐ no ☐ doesn't apply
- #2 ☐ yes ☐ no ☐ doesn't apply

9. **NDC #** (for product problems only)
– –

10. **Concomitant medical products** and therapy dates (exclude treatment of event)

D. Suspect medical device

1. **Brand name**

2. **Type of device**

3. **Manufacturer name & address**

4. **Operator of device**
- ☐ health professional
- ☐ lay user/patient
- ☐ other: ____

5. **Expiration date** (mo/day/yr)

6.
model # ____
catalog # ____
serial # ____
lot # ____
other #

7. **If implanted, give date** (mo/day/yr)

8. **If explanted, give date** (mo/day/yr)

9. **Device available for evaluation?** (Do not send to FDA)
☐ yes ☐ no ☐ returned to manufacturer on ____ (mo/day/yr)

10. **Concomitant medical products** and therapy dates (exclude treatment of event)

E. Reporter (see confidentiality section on back)

1. **Name, address & phone #**

2. **Health professional?** ☐ yes ☐ no

3. **Occupation**

4. **Also reported to**
- ☐ manufacturer
- ☐ user facility
- ☐ distributor

5. If you do NOT want your identity disclosed to the manufacturer, place an " X " in this box. ☐

FDA

Mail to: MEDWATCH
5600 Fishers Lane
Rockville, MD 20852-9787

or **FAX to:**
1-800-FDA-0178

FDA Form 3500 (6/93)   Submission of a report does not constitute an admission that medical personnel or the product caused or contributed to the event.

Form 6. STUDY SITE TELEPHONE LOG

Date _____ Time _____

Conversation With _____

Affiliation _____

Telephone # _____

Regarding (Product, Study #, Subject #) _____

        ❑ I Placed Call   ❑ I Returned Call

        ❑ Party Called   ❑ Party Returned Call

_____

_____

_____

_____

_____

_____

_____

_____

_____

Is action or follow-up necessary?   ❑ No   ❑ Yes (specify) _____

_____

_____

_____

Was action taken?   ❑ No   ❑ Yes (specify) _____

_____

_____

_____

Date filed in study file _____

Signed _____

    cc: _____

        _____

        _____

Form 7. STUDY ADVERTISEMENT OFFICE SIGN

DO YOU HAVE [*insert study indication here*]?

If you are between the ages of _____ and _____ years, and you have been diagnosed with _____ or have any of the following symptoms on a frequent basis:

- _____
- _____
- _____
- _____
- _____

- _____
- _____
- _____
- _____
- _____

[*list signs and symptoms of disease/indication being studied*]

then you may qualify for entry into a medical research program. Please contact a nurse, receptionist, or your doctor for more information regarding this free program.

Note: IRB and Sponsor approval are required before posting signs in public areas.

Form 8. SCREEN VISIT LETTER

(Note: Print on site letterhead stationery.)

Date:

RE: Protocol #

Dear _____:

This letter is to confirm our conversation regarding your potential participation in the above referenced research study being performed at our office. This study will involve people who have a diagnosis of _____. Your screening visit is scheduled for _____ at _____, with _____.

After you have reviewed the informed consent, had all your questions answered, and have agreed to participate in this clinical trial, you will be required to: (list the study requirements here). *(Note: It is important that no study-related procedures be performed prior to the signing of the informed consent, e.g., fasting for baseline laboratory samples, wash-out of restricted medications.)*

Your participation in this clinical trial is greatly appreciated. If you have any questions regarding your potential participation in this study, do not hesitate to contact me directly at _____. I look forward to meeting with you.

Sincerely,

_____
Clinical Research Study Coordinator

Form 9. BASELINE VISIT COVER LETTER

(Note: Print on site letterhead stationery.)

Date:

RE: Protocol #

Dear _____:

This letter is to confirm the date and time of your baseline visit for participation in the _____ research study. Your appointment has been scheduled for _____ at _____, with _____.

During your baseline visit, you will be required to undergo the following study procedures: *(Note: Some examples of study-related procedures)*

- ✔ complete physical exam;
- ✔ ECG;
- ✔ provide laboratory specimens; and
- ✔ chest radiograph.

In addition, you must fast for at least ___ hours prior to having your blood drawn. This means you may not have any food or drink (including water) for the given specified time period before your scheduled appointment. A sample of your urine will be obtained as well.

I look forward to working with you on this research study. If you have any questions about your participation in this research study, please do not hesitate to contact me at _____.

Your participation in this clinical trial is greatly appreciated.

Sincerely,

_____
Clinical Research Coordinator

Form 10. ONGOING STUDY VISIT LETTER

(Note: Print on site letterhead stationery.)

Date:

RE: Protocol #

Dear _____:

This is to confirm your next clinic visit for the _____ study on _____ at
_____, with _____.

During this visit, you will be required to undergo the following study-related procedures:
(Note: List study-specific procedures here.)

Should you need to take any medication other than the study medication between your first
and subsequent visit, you will be asked to keep a record of the dates, the dosages, and reason for
the medication so you may report them to me during your clinic visit. In addition, should you
experience any unpleasant side effects, you need to keep a record of what they are, when they
started, and how long they lasted so you may also report them to me during your clinic visit.

It is important that you remember to bring with you to this visit all unused study medication, including
the box and empty blister packs and study supplies, along with your patient diary (if applicable).

It is extremely important that you keep your scheduled clinic visit. If for some reason you are unable
to keep this appointment, kindly contact me immediately so that we can reschedule the appointment
according to the study guidelines.

Thank you for your continued participation in this research study. In the meantime, please do not
hesitate to contact me at (___)_____ if you have any questions or require additional information.

Sincerely,

_____
Clinical Research Coordinator

Form 11. FINAL STUDY LETTER

(Note: Print on site letterhead stationery.)

Date:

RE: Protocol #

Dear _____:

Dr. _____ and I would like to take this opportunity to express our sincere appreciation for your participation in Protocol _____

_____.

Without participants like you, clinical research would not be possible.

Please do not hesitate to contact me in the future if you have any questions regarding your participation in this research study. Again, thank you for your participation.

Sincerely,

_____
Clinical Research Coordinator

_____
Principal Investigator

Form 12. GENERIC FINANCIAL DISCLOSURE CERTIFICATION FORM

Principal Investigator's Name _____

Protocol # _____

Investigational Product _____

IND # _____

With respect to the clinical study for the investigational product referenced above that I am conducting for (*insert sponsoring pharmaceutical company's name*), I hereby certify to the truth and accuracy of the following statements in compliance with 21 CFR part 54, with the understanding that I am certifying not only for myself as a clinical investigator, but also for my spouse and for each dependent child of mine:

I certify that:

> ✔ I have not entered into any financial arrangement with (*insert sponsoring pharmaceutical company's name*) (e.g., bonus, royalty, or other financial incentive) whereby the outcome of the clinical study could affect my compensation;

> ✔ I do not have a proprietary interest (e.g., patent, trademark, copyright, licensing agreement, etc.) in the investigational product tested in the above referenced clinical study;

> ✔ I do not have a significant equity interest (e.g., any ownership interest, stock option, or other financial interest, the value of which cannot be calculated with reference to publicly available prices) in (*insert sponsoring pharmaceutical company's name*); and

> ✔ I have not received significant payments from (*insert sponsoring pharmaceutical company's name*), on or after February 2, 1999, having a total value in excess of $25,000, other than payments for conducting the clinical study. Examples of such significant payments include, but are not limited to, grants or funding for ongoing research, compensation in the form of equipment, retainers for ongoing consultation and honoraria that are (a) paid directly to me or to the institution with which I am affiliated, and (b) in support of my activities.

or

I disclose the following *(check all boxes that apply and attach detailed information):*

> ❑ I have entered into a financial arrangement with (*insert sponsoring pharmaceutical company's name*), whereby the value of my compensation could be influenced by the outcome of the clinical study;

110

❑ I am receiving significant payments from (*insert sponsoring pharmaceutical company's name*) on or after February 2, 1999, having value in excess of $25,000, other than payment for conducting the above clinical study. Examples of significant payments include, but are not limited to, grants or funding for ongoing research, compensation in the form of equipment, retainers for ongoing consultation and honoraria that are (a) paid directly to me or to the institution with which I am affiliated, and (b) paid in support of my activities;

❑ I hold a proprietary interest (e.g., patent, trademark, copyright, licensing agreement, etc.) in the investigational product being tested in the clinical study; and

❑ I have a significant equity interest (e.g., any ownership interest, stock option, or other financial interest, the value of which cannot be calculated with reference to publicly available prices) in (*insert sponsoring pharmaceutical company's name*).

This certification shall apply throughout the entire term of the clinical study and for one year following completion of the clinical study. If there is any change in the accuracy of the foregoing statements during such time period, I shall hereby agree that I will promptly notify (*insert sponsoring pharmaceutical company's name*).

_____

Signature of Principal Investigator   Date

*Tax ID#/Social Security # _____

Affiliated Institution _____

Tax ID# _____

Required for internal tracking only and will not be submitted to the FDA.

Form 13. Sample HIPAA Authorization to Access Protected Health Information

Protocol Title _____

Protocol # _____

Sponsor _____

Principal Investigator's Name _____

✔ Access to your Protected Health Information ("PHI") will be required for the purpose of your participation in this research study.

✔ PHI is medical information that identifies you as an individual, such as name, address, social security number, and other personal details about you.

✔ This will include information, which is used to determine your eligibility for the research study and collected from the procedures that are carried out as part of the research study. This may include the following types of personal information:

1. Your past medical history, including medical information from your primary care physician

2. Physical exam, laboratory tests (blood and/or urine)

3. Response to any study treatments you may receive

4. Information related to study visits and phone calls

5. Additional tests or procedures required by the protocol

6. Other information relating to your participation in this research study (include any study specific information, i.e., x-ray, EKG, will need to be added here)

✔ With your permission, the Principal Investigator (study physician) and his research staff will be allowed to give this information to the research study Sponsor's key individuals. The Sponsor's key individuals include any person or company working for or with the Sponsor to facilitate the research study. They will have the right to see your health information and know your identity during and after the research study.

✔ These key individuals agree to keep all of your information confidential, which will minimize the risk that it will be released to others without your permission.

✔ Permission to access your protected health information will continue until such time as it is no longer required by the Sponsor of this research study.

✔ You have the right to see and copy any of the information gathered about you, but not until the research study is completed.

✔ You also have the right to withdraw this permission at any time by providing a ***written request*** to the research study physician. When you withdraw your permission, no new health information that might identify you will be gathered after that date and you will not be able to continue participation in the research study. Information that has already been obtained may still be used by the Sponsor.

✔ By signing this authorization form, you are giving your permission to use and give out your protected health information. If you do not give your permission, you will not be able to continue in this research study.

✔ You will be provided with a copy of this form for your personal files.

_____

Signature of Subject   Date

_____

Signature of Legally Authorized Representative (if applicable)   Date

_____

Authority of Subject's Personal Representative or Relationship to Subject
(when signed by a Legally Authorized Representative)

STOP!

BEFORE ANY MED CHANGES
KINDLY CONTACT:

(INSERT NAME AND NUMBER OF PERSON RESPONSIBLE)

THIS PATIENT IS A PARTICIPANT
IN A RESEARCH PROJECT

STOP!

THIS PATIENT IS A PARTICIPANT IN A RESEARCH PROJECT

KINDLY CONTACT:
(INSERT NAME AND NUMBER OF PERSON RESPONSIBLE)

REGARDING THE FOLLOWING:
✔ PRIOR TO ANY CHANGES TO CURRENT MEDICATION

✔ <u>ANY</u> CHANGES IN THE PATIENT'S PHYSICAL CONDITION

✔ DATE AND TIME PATIENT WILL BE DISCHARGED

Form 16. Transporting Study Material from Main Site to Satellite Sites

Protocol Number: _____ Sponsor: _____

To Be Dispensed at Satellite Office

Site Location: _____

Principal Investigator: _____

Research Nurse: _____

Subject Initials: _____   Subject Number: _____

Lot Number: _____   Amount of Study Drug Sent: _____

Temperature at Packaging: _____   Time Sent: _____

Special Instructions: _____

_____

_____   _____
Signature of Person Transferring to Courier   Date

_____   _____
Signature of Research Nurse Receiving Study Drug   Date

Time Study Drug Received: _____   Temperature at Receipt: _____

SIGN AND FAX THIS FORM IMMEDIATELY UPON RECEIPT OF STUDY DRUG TO:

_____

Store Study Drug According to Instructions Noted on Form
Place Copy of This Form in Your Research Drug Accountability Log
RETURN OF UNUSED STUDY DRUG FROM SATELLITE OFFICE

_____   _____
Signature of Research Nurse Returning Unused Medication   Date

Amount Returned*: _____   Time Returned: _____

_____   _____
Signature of Person Receiving Returned Medication   Date

Amount Received*: _____   Time Received: _____
(i.e.: bottles; vials; blister packs)

_____   _____
Signature of Research Nurse Verifying Return Study Drug Accountability   Date

Form 17. PRINCIPAL INVESTIGATOR DELEGATION OF RESPONSIBILITIES

PRINCIPAL INVESTIGATOR DELEGATION OF RESPONSIBILITIES

Sponsor: _____

Study Title: _____

Study #: _____

Principal Investigator: _____

Site Name: _____

Site Number: _____

List the names, signatures, initials and procedure responsibilities for those individuals participating in the conduct of this trial

Procedures Responsibilities Legend (For Reference Only)

1. Physical
2. History
3. Phlebotomy
4. Collecting Safety Data
5. Collecting Efficacy Data
6. Dispense Medication(s)
7. CRF Entry
8. Scheduling Study Visits
9. Performing Special Study Procedures

Name and Title (please print)	Listed on 1572?	Signature	Initials	Procedure Responsibilities (Enter Applicable Number(s) from Above)	Date(s)
Name: Title:	☐ No ☐ Yes				
Name: Title:	☐ No ☐ Yes				
Name: Title:	☐ No ☐ Yes				
Name: Title:	☐ No ☐ Yes				
Name: Title:	☐ No ☐ Yes				

APPENDIX III: Individual State Regulatory Requirements for Conducting a Clinical Trial Using an Investigational Drug

FDA District Offices

Food and Drug Administration (FDA) District Offices are located throughout the country. IRB and other inspections are conducted by FDA District Office personnel. Problems or questions related to FDA-regulated products or IRB inspections may be directed to the Director of the Investigations Branch (unless otherwise indicated), or the Bioresearch Monitoring Program Coordinator, in the appropriate District Office.

DISTRICT	STATES SERVED
ATLANTA District 60 Eighth Street, N.E. Atlanta, Georgia 30309 (404) 347-3218	Georgia, North Carolina, South Carolina
BALTIMORE District 900 Madison Avenue Baltimore, Maryland 21201-2199 (410) 962-3590	District of Columbia, Maryland, Virginia, West Virginia
NEW ENGLAND District One Montvale Avenue Stoneham, Massachusetts 02180 (617) 279-1675, EXT 128	Connecticut, Maine, Massachusetts, New Hampshire, Rhode Island, Vermont
BUFFALO District 599 Delaware Avenue Buffalo, New York 14202 (716) 551 44 61	New York (except New York City, Long Island)
CHICAGO District 300 S. Riverside Plaza 5th Floor, Suite 550 South Chicago, Illinois 60606 (312) 353-5863 EXT 132	Illinois
CINCINNATI District 1141 Central Parkway Cincinnati, Ohio 45202-1097 (513) 684-3501 EXT 130	Ohio, Kentucky
DALLAS District 3310 Live Oak St. Dallas, Texas 75204 (214) 655-5310 EXT 504	Arkansas, Oklahoma, Texas
DENVER District P.O. Box 25087 6th and Kipling Sts. Denver Federal Center Denver, Colorado 80225-0087 (303) 236-3051	Colorado, New Mexico, Utah

DISTRICT	STATES SERVED
DETROIT District 1560 East Jefferson Detroit, Michigan 4 8207-3179 (313) 226-6260	Indiana, Michigan
FLORIDA District 555 Winderley Place Maitland, Florida 32751 (4 07) 4 754 700	Florida
KANSAS CITY, District 11630 West 80th St. Lenexa, Kansas 66285-5905 (913) 752-24 23	Iowa, Kansas, Missouri, Nebraska
LOS ANGELES District 19900 MacArthur Blvd., Suite 300 Irvine, California 92612-244 5 (714) 798-7769	Arizona, California (southern)
MINNEAPOLIS District 24 0 Hennepin Avenue Minneapolis, Minnesota 554 01-1912 (612) 334 4 100 EXT 162	Minnesota, Wisconsin, North Dakota, South Dakota
NASHVILLE District 297 Plus Park Boulevard Nashville, Tennessee 37217 (615) 781-5378	Alabama, Tennessee
NEW JERSEY District Waterview Corp. Center 10 Waterway Bend, 3rd Floor Parsippany, New Jersey 07054 (201) 526-6000	New Jersey
NEW ORLEANS District 4 298 Elysian Fields Avenue New Orleans, Louisiana 70122 (504) 589-6344	Louisiana, Mississippi
NEW YORK District 850 Third Avenue Brooklyn, New York 11232-1593 (718) 34 0-7000	New York City, Long Island
PHILADELPHIA District 2nd and Chestnut Streets Room 900 Philadelphia, Pennsylvania 19106 (215) 597-4 390	Delaware, Pennsylvania

DISTRICT	STATES SERVED
SEATTLE District 22201 23rd Drive S.E. P.O. Box 3012 Bothell, Washington 98041-3012 (206) 483 4941	Alaska, Idaho, Oregon, Montana, Washington
SAN FRANCISCO District 1431 Harbor Bay Parkway Alameda, California 94502-7070 (510) 337-6733	California (northern), Hawaii, Nevada, American Samoa, Guam, Pacific Trust Territory
SAN JUAN District #466 Fernandez Juncos Avenue Stop 8 1/2 San Juan, Puerto Rico 00901-3223 (809) 729-6608	Puerto Rico

APPENDIX IV: Conversion Tables

A. Conversion to Military Time

Military time is simple and logical. It is based on the fact that each day is composed of 24 hours numbered from 1 through 24. As with conventional time, the last two digits of military time are used to indicate the minute after the hour. For example, the conventional times 6:30 AM and 11:45 PM would be written in military times as 0630 and 2345, respectively.

1:00 AM	= 0100	1:00 PM	= 1300
2:00 AM	= 0200	2:00 PM	= 1400
3:00 AM	= 0300	3:00 PM	= 1500
4:00 AM	= 0400	4:00 PM	= 1600
5:00 AM	= 0500	5:00 PM	= 1700
6:00 AM	= 0600	6:00 PM	= 1800
7:00 AM	= 0700	7:00 PM	= 1900
8:00 AM	= 0800	8:00 PM	= 2000
9:00 AM	= 0900	9:00 PM	= 2100
10:00 AM	= 1000	10:00 PM	= 2200
11:00 AM	= 1100	11:00 PM	= 2300
12:00 PM	= 1200	12:00 AM	= 2400

IMPORTANT: Note that 12:00 midnight is written 2400 in military time. However, one never goes past 2400 hours. One minute past midnight becomes 0001, 30 minutes past midnight becomes 0030, etc., right up to 59 minutes past midnight, which is 0059. The time 1:00 AM then becomes 0100.

B. Measures and Equivalents

Volume

29.57 mL = 1 fluid ounce
473 mL = 1 pint
1 liter = 33.8 fluid ounces
3785 mL = 1 gallon
5 mL = 1 teaspoon
15 mL = 1 tablespoon or 1/2 fluid ounce

Weight

1 kilogram [kg] = 2.2 lbs.
1 pound = 453.59 grams
1 ounce = 28.35 grams
1 gram = 15.432 grains
1 grain = 65 mg
1/2 grain = 32.4 mg
1/4 grain = 16.2 mg

Height

1 centimeter [cm] = 0.39 inches
1 inch = 2.54 cm
1 meter = 39.37 inches
1 micron = 1/1000 mm

Other useful measures

1 liter of water weighs 1 kg
1 mL of water weighs 1 gram

C. Conversion Charts for Height and Weight Measurements

Feet Inches	Inches	Centimeters
4' 8"	56	142.2
4' 9"	57	144.8
4' 10"	58	147.3
4' 11"	59	149.9
5' 0"	60	152.4
5' 1"	61	154.9
5' 2"	62	157.5
5' 3"	63	160.0
5' 4"	64	162.6
5' 5"	65	165.1
5' 6"	66	167.6
5' 7"	67	170.2
5' 8"	68	172.7
5' 9"	69	175.3
5' 10"	70	177.8
5' 11"	71	180.3
6' 0"	72	182.9
6' 1"	73	185.4
6' 2"	74	188.0
6' 3"	75	190.5
6' 4"	76	193.0
6' 5"	77	195.6
6' 6"	78	198.1
6' 7"	79	200.7
6' 8"	80	203.2

Pounds	Kilograms
1	0.4535
2.2046	1.0
95	43.1
100	45.4
105	47.6
110	49.9
115	52.2
120	54.4
125	56.7
130	59.0
135	61.2
140	63.5
145	65.8
150	68.0
155	70.3
160	72.6
165	74.8
170	77.1
175	79.4
180	81.6
185	83.9
190	86.2
195	88.5
200	90.7
205	93.0
210	95.3
215	97.5
220	99.8
225	102.1
230	104.3
235	106.6
240	108.9
245	111.1
250	113.4
255	115.7
260	117.9
265	120.2
270	122.5
275	124.7
280	127.0
285	129.3
290	131.5
295	133.8
300	136.1

Appendix V: Common Terms and Acronyms

Acronym	Term
ADME	Absorption, Distribution, Metabolized, Excretion
ADR/AE	Adverse Drug Reaction/Adverse Event
CDA	Confidentiality Disclosure Agreement
CDM	Clinical Data Management
CFR	Code of Federal Regulations
CNS	Central Nervous System
CRA	Clinical Research Associate
CRO	Contract Research Organization
CRF	Case Report Form
CRS	Clinical Regulatory Specialist
DEA	Drug Enforcement Administration
EC	Ethics Committee
GCP	Good Clinical Practice
GLP	Good Laboratory Practice
HREC	Human Research Ethics Committees
HMO	Health Management Organization
IB	Investigator Brochure
IC	Informed Consent

ICF	Informed Consent Form
ICH	International Conference on Harmonization
IEC	Independent Ethics Committee
IRB	Institutional Review Board
IRDB	Investigator Research Database
ISFN	Investigator Site File Notebook
LOI	Letter of Intent
LREC	Local Research Ethics Committee
MAP	Master Action Plan
MREC	Multi Research Ethics Committee (UK)
NDA	New Drug Application
PI	Principal Investigator
PIS	Patient Information Sheet
PM	Project Manager
PQRS	PPD Query Resolution System
QA	Quality Assurance
QC	Quality Control
RA	Research Assistant
RCM	Research Coordination Manager
RCR	Regulatory Compliance Review
RTMS	Research Trial Management System™

SAE	Serious Adverse Event
SC	Study Coordinator
SMF	Study Master File
SMO	Site Management Organization
SOP	Standard Operating Procedures
TAL	Training Attendance Log
TMF	Trial Master File
WHO	World Health Organization

APPENDIX VI: Glossary of Terms

Abbreviated New Drug Application (ANDA)
Simplified submission for products with the same or very closely related active ingredients, dosage form, use, strength, administration route, and labeling as a product that has already been shown to be safe and effective. An ANDA includes all the information on chemistry and manufacturing controls found in an NDA, but does not usually have to include efficacy and safety data from studies in animals and humans. It must, however, contain evidence that the duplicate drug is bioequivalent to the previously approved drug.

Administrative Change
Change to a protocol involving only administrative details and having no impact on study design or subject safety. An administrative change requires IRB/IEC notification, but does not require notification of regulatory agencies prior to implementation.

Adverse Event (AE)
An AE is any untoward medical occurrence in a patient or clinical investigation subject administered a pharmaceutical product and that does not necessarily have a causal relationship with this treatment. An AE can therefore be any unfavorable and unintended sign (including an abnormal laboratory finding), symptom, or disease temporarily associated with the use of a medicinal (investigational) product, whether or not related to the medicinal (investigational) product. (See the ICH Guideline for Clinical Safety Data Management: Definitions and Standards for Expedited Reporting.) (ICH)

Altered Data
Generating biased data or changed data that is legitimately obtained. An example of an altered document includes unsupported changes to data on a document, such as exam dates, date of birth, etc. An example of altered data can include unsupported changes to data in the source document and/or the case report form.

Amended Protocol
A protocol that has been revised or an amendment to the Protocol.

ANDA
Abbreviated New Drug Application

ANDA Protocol Outline
Document that defines study design, reference formulation, and basic pharmacokinetics of compound to be tested.

Application Application is a formal request for review and approval, where issue of an opinion/approval by the regulatory authority is required for the trial commencement.

Archival The process of performing a full backup of a project's study data, metadata, and associated files to tape for long-term storage at an offsite facility.

ARSAC Administration of Radioactive Substances Advisory Committee

Audit A systematic and independent examination of trial-related activities and documents to determine whether the evaluated trial-related activities were conducted, and whether the data was recorded, analyzed, and accurately reported according to the Protocol, Sponsor's standard operating procedures (SOPs), Good Clinical Practice (GCP) and the applicable regulatory requirement(s). (ICH GCP 1.6)

Audit-Related Documents Written evaluations by a regulatory agency or a quality assurance group (internal or external) that contain findings and observations about PPD activities.

Author Person writing any section of the Investigator Brochure. May be a member of the medical writing, clinical pharmacology, medical affairs, or regulatory affairs staff.

Becquerel (Bq) Radiological unit, source strength

Bind To place yourself under legal obligation and/or to cause you to be legally responsible.

Blinding/Masking A procedure in which one or more parties to the trial are kept unaware of the treatment assignment(s). Single-blinding usually refers to the subject(s) being unaware, and double-blinding usually refers to the subject(s), investigator(s), monitor, and, in some cases, data analyst(s) being unaware of the treatment assignment(s). (ICH)

Blood Means human blood, human blood components, and products made from human blood.

Bloodborne Pathogens Means pathogenic microorganisms that are present in human blood and can cause disease in humans. These pathogens include, but are not limited to, HBV virus (HBV) and human immunodeficiency virus (HIV).

BMI (Body Mass Index) This is a value obtained when weight is divided by height. The formula used for calculation of this value is BMI = Weight (Kg) / Height (m) x Height (m).

Call Center Services (CCS) The area where the telephone operators use computers and telephone equipment to assist in subject/site recruitment and/or site support programs.

Call Center Services Questionnaire The combined document of standardized opening remarks relative to the nature of clinical research, research subject rights, and confidentiality along with standardized study specific questions used to collect data from potential subjects; sometimes referred to as "script" or "transcript."

Call Center Services Site Participating institutions or clinics that have provided documentation of respective advertisement approval, as needed, and that are Sponsor- or Clincal Operations-approved recipients of CCS efforts.

Call Center Services Staff (Operators) Personnel who receive and record information by telephone from prospective study subjects and/or consumers pursuant to CCS advertising and recruitment programs.

Call Report For purposes of this procedure, record of a specific Technical Support Communication. Use of the word "call" does not imply that these reports originate exclusively from telephone contact.

Case Report Form (CRF) A printed, optical, or electronic document designed to record all of the protocol-required information to be reported to the sponsor on each trial subject. (ICH)

Casebook Guide Instructions for completing the CRF that may include sample completed CRF pages.

Causality Relationship of an investigational product to an AE. Many causality categories are used to describe the degree of attributability of a product to an AE, such as Definite, Probable, Possible, Remote, Not Related; however, currently, there is no standard nomenclature.

Central Laboratory	Primary laboratory used by all investigators participating in a study for the analysis of specimens (e.g., biological fluids and tissue).
Centralized Recruitment Program	A specific recruitment campaign consisting of one or more advertising media and support materials directed to either potential research subjects, or consumers.
Certified Copy	An exact copy of the original with initial and date of individual making the copy from the original with a statement that this is a true exact copy.
CFR	Code of Federal Regulations
Clinical Data Management	Department responsible for managing database generation through data entry, data review, and data clean-up using data collected from a clinical study.
Clinical Monitor	The person responsible for monitoring the conduct and progress of the clinical trial.
Clinical Research Associate (CRA)	Appropriately trained sponsor representative or contracted individual who is responsible for overseeing the conduct of a clinical study. The CRA makes periodic visits to the trial site before, during, and at the conclusion of a study, to ascertain that the clinical protocol is being adhered to and that all aspects of Good Clinical Practice are followed. Also synonymous with monitor.
Clinical Trial Materials	Articles used in the conduct of a clinical trial, excluding investigational product. (Examples of clinical trial materials are CRFs, patient diaries, laboratory kits, thermometers.)
Clinical Trial/Study	Any investigation in human subjects intended to discover or verify the clinical, pharmacological, and/or other pharmacodynamic effects of an investigational product(s), and/or to identify any adverse reactions to an investigational product(s), and/or to study absorption, distribution, metabolism, and excretion of an investigational product(s) with the object of ascertaining its safety and/or efficacy. The terms "clinical trial" and "clinical study" are synonymous. (ICH)
Clinical Trial/Study Report	A written description of a trial/study of any therapeutic, prophylactic, or diagnostic agent conducted in human subjects, in

which the clinical and statistical description, presentations, and analyses are fully integrated into a single report. (See the ICH Guideline for Structure and Content of Clinical Study Reports.)

Clintrial Database Administrator
The individual who provides user support and administration, security, and other operational support for Clintrial database activities.

Co-investigators
Investigators having equal power and responsibilities for a clinical trial.

Communications
Communications include written, verbal, or electronic communication such as, but not limited to, letters, memoranda, facsimile transmissions, electronic mail messages, voice mail messages, telephone conversations, and meetings.

Compassionate Use
Sometimes used to describe a request by a practitioner to treat a single patient with an investigational product. The request is usually in response to a desperate situation, such as the lack of approved or generally recognized treatments or the patient being unresponsive to other therapies.

Computer System Validation
Documented evidence, to a high degree of assurance, that the computer system performs its intended functions accurately and reliably.

Confidentiality
Prevention of disclosure, to other than authorized individuals, and/or Sponsor's propriety information or of a subject's identity. (ICH derived)

Confidentiality Agreement
Document preventing disclosure of facts to third parties. Also synonymous with Secrecy Agreement.

Contact Report
Written record of contact between a Sponsor's employee and trial site staff, client company, contract service agency, or regulatory agency.

Contaminated Laundry
Laundry that has been soiled with blood, body fluids, or other potentially infectious materials.

Contaminated Sharps
Any contaminated object that can penetrate the skin including, but not limited to, needles, scalpels, broken glass, broken capillary tubes, and exposed ends of dental wires.

Contamination	The presence or the reasonably anticipated presence of blood or other potentially infectious materials on an item or surface.
Contract Research Organization (CRO)	A person or an organization (commercial, academic, or other) contracted by the sponsor to perform one or more of a Sponsor's trial-related duties and functions. (ICH GCP 1.20)
Debarment	The FDA, authorized by the U.S. Generic Drug Enforcement Act (1992), has the right to forbid or deny individuals and/or firms from participation in the development of an investigational product. Those individuals/firms having been debarred are published in the U.S. Federal Register.
Declaration of Helsinki	International document defining the ethical principles under which clinical research is to be conducted.
Decontamination	The use of physical or chemical means to remove, inactivate, and destroy bloodborne pathogens. Pathogens must be destroyed on a surface or item to the point where they are no longer capable of transmitting infectious particles and the surface or item is rendered safe for handling, use, or disposal.
Deliverable	Any report text, table, listing, and figure or database produced for delivery to the client.
Designee	Individual empowered to sign agreements or perform actions through their position in an organization.
Dispensing Investigational Product	The act of providing investigational product to a subject wherein the study personnel inject, apply, or observe the physical administration of investigational product on or by the subject.
Dosing	The act of providing a unit dose or applying an investigational product to a subject wherein the study personnel inject, apply, or observe the physical administration of the investigational product on or by the subject.
Dosing Error	When an incorrect dose of investigational product has been inadvertently given to a subject, or taken by a subject, including dispensing or administering to the wrong subject or taking/administering the study medication on the wrong day or time, having taken/administered the wrong investigational product.

Drug Enforcement Administration (DEA)	Lead agency in the U.S. responsible for enforcing the controlled substance laws and regulations of the U.S.
Exposure Incident	A specific eye, mouth, other mucous membrane, nonintact skin, or parenteral contact with blood or other potentially infectious materials that result from the performance of an employee's duties.
FDA	Food and Drug Administration
Financial Agreement	Document containing details of all financial arrangements entered into between the client company and/or a trial site. The financial agreement may form part of the Study Site Agreement (e.g., Statement of Agreement).
Fraud	Deliberate reporting of false or misleading data or the withholding of reportable data. Fraud does not include the submitting of poor quality data without the intent to deceive.
Good Clinical Practice (GCP)	A standard for the design, conduct, performance, monitoring, auditing, recording, analyses, and reporting of clinical trials that provides assurance that the data and reported results are credible and accurate, and that the rights, integrity, and confidentiality of trial subjects are protected. (ICH)
Hand-Washing Facilities	A facility providing an adequate supply of running potable water, soap, and single-use towels or hot air drying machines.
HAV	Hepatitis A Virus.
HBV	Hepatitis B Virus.
HCV	Hepatitis C Virus
HIV	Human Immunodeficiency Virus, the causative agent in Acquired Immune Deficiency Syndrome (AIDS).
ICH	International Conference on the Harmonization of Technical Requirements for registration of Pharmaceuticals for Human Use—a group of worldwide regulatory agencies and professional trade organizations formed to provide global standards for pharmaceutical development in the U.S., Europe, and Japan.
IND	Investigational New Drug Application

IND Study

Study conducted in accordance with the requirements of the FDA (Food and Drug Administration) Investigational New Drug regulations.

Indemnification

Process to relieve the investigator, subinvestigators, IRB/IEC, and/or research institution of responsibility against hurt, loss, or damage to subjects resulting from participation in a clinical trial.

Independent Ethics Committee (IEC)

An independent body (a review board or a committee, institutional, regional, national, or supranational), constituted of medical/scientific professionals and nonmedical/nonscientific members, whose responsibility it is to ensure the protection of the rights, safety, and well-being of human subjects involved in a trial and to provide public assurance of that protection, by, among other things, reviewing and approving/providing favorable opinion on the trial protocol, the suitability of the investigator(s), facilities, and the methods and material to be used in obtaining and documenting informed consent of the trial subjects. The legal status, composition, function, operations, and regulatory requirements pertaining to Independent Ethics Committees may differ among countries, but should allow the Independent Ethics Committee to act in agreement with GCP as described in this guideline. (ICH)

Informational Translation

Informational translations are used where the original document remains the reference document, but translations of all or part of it will assist other parties in the review of documents. Examples are the translation of all or part of the local Investigational Ethics Committee approval letter or an Investigator CV.

Informed Consent

A process by which a subject voluntarily confirms his or her willingness to participate in a particular trial, after having been informed of all aspects of the trial that are relevant to the subject's decision to participate. Informed consent is documented by means of a written, signed, and dated informed consent form. (ICH)

Informed Consent Document

Document prepared in nontechnical language to provide clinical trial subjects with information detailing trial procedures, potential benefits, risks and inconveniences, and the subject's rights. This document is used to obtain proof of the subject's agreement to enter a study.

Inspection

The act by a regulatory authority(ies) of conducting an official review of documents, facilities, records, and any other resources that are deemed by the authority(ies) to be related to the clinical trial and that may be located at the site of the trial, at the sponsor's and/or contract research organization's (CRO) facilities, or at other establishments deemed appropriate by the regulatory authority(ies). (ICH GCP 1.29)

Installation Qualification (IQ)

Documented evidence that installation instructions were followed for computer system hardware and/or software.

Institutional Review Board (IRB)

An independent body constituted of medical, scientific, and nonscientific members, whose responsibility it is to ensure the protection of the rights, safety, and well-being of human subjects involved in a trial by, among other things, reviewing, approving, and providing continuing review of trials, of protocols and amendments, and of the methods and material to be used in obtaining and documenting informed consent of the trial subjects. (ICH)

Interactive Voice Response System (IVRS)

Automated central randomization system allowing investigators to obtain subject randomization information by telephone by use of interactive voice technology or a touch-tone keypad. IVRS systems may also control distribution of investigational product to sites.

International Conference on Harmonization (ICH)

Group of worldwide regulatory agencies and professional trade organizations formed to provide harmonization of technical requirements for the development of pharmaceutical products.

Investigational New Drug Application (IND)

The application for an exemption from the U.S. Federal law requiring an approved NDA prior to shipping a drug in interstate commerce. The IND contains the clinical development plan for the drug, including as complete a picture as possible of the compound (e.g., structural formula), chemistry and manufacturing information, and the results of animal pharmacology and toxicology studies with the drug.

Investigational Product

A pharmaceutical form of an active ingredient or placebo being tested or used as a reference in a clinical trial, including a product with a market authorization when used or assembled (formulated or packaged) in a way different from the approved form, or when used for an unapproved indication, or when used to gain further information about an approved use. (ICH)

Investigational Product Labels

Labels attached to inner and outer containers of investigational products containing all information sufficient to identify the product and meet local regulations for such products.

Investigational Product Release	Regulatory compliance personnel's authorization to ship investigational product.
Investigator	One or more persons responsible for the practical performance of a clinical trial and for the integrity, health, and welfare of the subjects during the trial. The investigator is an appropriately qualified, trained, and experienced person, particularly in the clinical area of the proposed trial, who is familiar with the background and the requirements of the study. If a trial is conducted by a team of individuals at a trial site, the investigator is the responsible leader of the team and may be called the principal investigator.
Investigator Meeting	Meeting to provide training to investigators and other trial site staff on all aspects of a clinical study.
Investigator Site File	File that is prepared for or by the investigator prior to study initiation and contains copies of documents relating to the clinical study. It is kept at the trial site, updated by the investigator and reviewed by the monitor at the monitoring visits. It must be retained by the investigator for a fixed period after the study is completed. Also known as Site Regulatory Binder or Regulatory Binder.
Investigator's Brochure	A compilation of the clinical and nonclinical data on the investigational product(s) that is relevant to the study of the investigational product(s) in human subjects. The information must be updated during the course of the clinical program, as new data are generated. (ICH derived)
IRMER	Ionising Radiation (Medical Exposure) Regulations (2000).
Laboratory	A workplace where diagnostic or other screening procedures are performed on blood or other potentially infectious materials.
Licensed Healthcare Professional	A person whose legally permitted scope of practice allows him or her to independently perform the activities required.
Manufactured or Fabricated Data	Data or information created without performing the tasks required to get the data. This includes data that is not supported by the presence of reasonably expected source documentation. An example of a fabricated document includes a document that has been created and submitted for a particular study subject, but that does not actually belong to that subject and lacks source documentation for items such as lab findings, chest x-rays, and concomitant medications.

Meaningful Pain Relief The time point at which the patient feels that they have had a significant amount of pain relief post dose.

Monitor See Clinical Research Associate.

Monitoring The act of overseeing the progress of a clinical trial, and of ensuring that it is conducted, recorded, and reported in accordance with the protocol, standard operating procedures (SOPs), GCP, and the applicable regulatory requirement(s). (ICH)

Multicenter Trial/Study A clinical trial conducted according to a single protocol but at more than one site, and, therefore, carried out by more than one investigator. (ICH)

NDA New Drug Application

Needleless Systems Devices that do not use needles for administration of medication or fluids or collection of blood or body fluids after initial access is established.

New Drug Application (NDA) Application requesting FDA approval to market a new drug for human use.

Notification Notification is the act of giving notice or information to the regulatory authority, but where review of documents or issue of an opinion/approval by the authority is not required for trial commencement (an acknowledgment of receipt may be provided).

Obligations Responsibilities for aspects of the control, management, and conduct of a clinical trial.

Occupational Exposure Reasonably anticipated skin, eye, mucous membrane, or parenteral contact with blood or other potentially infectious materials that may result from the performance of an employee's duties.

Omitted Data Data that has an impact on the study outcome and is not reported to the CRF. An example of omitted data includes the failure to correctly report exclusion criteria.

Pain Relief Scale A categorical scale (none, a little, some, a lot, complete) for indicating the level of pain relief being experienced by a patient.

Pain Scale A categorical scale (none, mild, moderate, severe) for indicating the level of pain being experienced by a patient.

Perceptible Pain Relief The time point at which the patient feels that they first perceive pain relief post dose.

Potential Investigator Individual who is being considered to conduct a clinical trial.

Potentially Infectious Material Blood or body fluid that may potentially contain a bloodborne pathogen, such as blood or semen, vaginal secretions, cerebrospinal fluid, synovial fluid, pleural fluid, peritoneal fluid, amniotic fluid, or pericardial fluid. Saliva or any body fluid or tissue where it is difficult or impossible to determine contamination must also be considered infectious.

Procedural Documents Standard Operating Procedures

Program Any activity associated with a Protocol, consisting of advertising media and/or support materials directed to potential research subjects, CCS sites, or consumers.

Program Files Consist of documents pertaining to the conduct of a CCS program, including, but not limited to final IRB/IEC approved Protocol/advertisements, final approved screening questionnaires, internal/external communication and CCS training/QA documentation, and are stored in the CCS file room and serve as an archive for all program-specific information.

Program Manager Individual who directs a drug development program that may include many separate projects.

Project The evaluation of a company or other entity for potential merger, acquisition, strategic joint venture, or other similar form of collaboration.

Project Manager Individual functionally responsible for the coordination and management of activities associated with all or part of a project.

Project-Specific Documents Extensive working instructions or comprehensive procedures applicable to certain projects, tasks, or locations.

Project Team	Assigned representatives from each functional group involved in performing the project workscope (e.g., Biostatistics, Data Management, Clinical, PVG, Regulatory, and Medical Writing).
Proprietary	Information or product that is owned by an individual or company that may be protected under a copyright or patent. Such information is considered to be a trade secret and is not to be disseminated without the written consent of the individual or company.
Protocol	A document that describes the objective(s), design, methodology, statistical considerations, and organization of a trial. The protocol usually also gives the background and rationale for the trial, but these could be provided in other Protocol referenced documents. Throughout the ICH GCP Guideline, the term Protocol refers to Protocol and Protocol amendments. (ICH)
Protocol Amendment	Change to a clinical Protocol that affects the safety of subjects, the scope of the investigation, or the scientific quality of the study. Requires IRB/IEC approval, and notification and/or approval of regulatory agencies prior to implementation.
Protocol Author	Individual responsible for coordinating development of a clinical Protocol.
Protocol Number	Unique identifying code for a clinical Protocol.
Protocol Violation	Failure to comply with the Protocol that results in a significant added risk to the subject; failure by the subject or investigator to adhere to significant (inclusion/exclusion/primary endpoint criteria defined by the clinical team) Protocol requirements yet the subject is enrolled and/or continuing in the study without prior client company approval; and noncompliance to Good Clinical Practice (FDA regulations and/or ICH GCP guidelines).
Quality Assurance	All those planned and systematic actions that are established to ensure that the trial is performed and the data are generated, documented (recorded), and reported in compliance with GCP and applicable regulatory requirements. (ICH)

Quality Control

The operational techniques and activities undertaken to verify that the requirements for quality of the trial-related activities have been fulfilled. (ICH derived)

Query

Request for the clarification of an item contained in a CRF (e.g., clarification of inaccuracy, discrepancy, or item requiring resolution).

Randomization

The process of assigning trial subjects to treatment or control groups using an element of chance to determine the assignments in order to reduce bias. (ICH)

Randomization Code

A schedule identifying the treatment each subject will receive during each study period while participating in a clinical trial.

Randomization Team

Individuals involved in the generation, receipt, storage, or distribution of randomization information. It must include at least one degreed statistician and at least one quality reviewer. Each team member must have a designated and comparably qualified backup. Randomization team members must not serve as project team members on any project where they also function as randomization team members.

Regulatory Agency Report

Notification of facts to a regulatory agency, which may be made periodically (e.g., annual updates) or as required (e.g., serious adverse event reporting).

Regulatory Authority

National body (e.g., Food and Drug Administration [FDA]; Medicines Control Agency [MCA]; Bundesinstitut für Arzneimittel und Medizinprodukte [BfArM]; Health Protection Branch [HPB], etc.) controlling the use and approval of medicinal products and devices.

Rescue Medication

The pain relief medication provided to the patient at their request if the patient does not achieve adequate pain relief from the study medication.

Research Agreement

Shall mean any agreement entered into between CRO/SMO or the client company and the investigator regarding a particular study. The Research Agreement shall set forth all obligations and services to be performed by the investigator in compensation therefore.

RPA

Radiation Protection Advisor

RPS	Radiation Protection Supervisor
Safety Monitor	Person responsible for the review and evaluation of information relevant to the safety of the drug (listed on Line 15 of the Form FDA 1571).
Safety Physician/Medical Monitor	A physician designated to be responsible for monitoring medical safety of the subjects in a given study, including, but not limited to, unblinding, AE reporting, and management.
Senior Statistical Reviewer	A senior statistician who performs experimental statistical review to ensure scientific integrity of all Biostatistics deliverables and the Study Report, as assigned by Biostatistics Management.
Serious Adverse Event/Experience (SAE) or Serious Adverse Drug Reaction (Serious ADR)	Any adverse drug experience occurring at any dose that results in any of the following outcomes: • death • life-threatening, that is, any event that (in the opinion of the Investigator) poses an immediate risk of death from that event • inpatient hospitalization • prolongation of existing hospitalization • persistent or significant disability/incapacity • congenital anomaly/birth defect Important medical events that may not result in death, be life-threatening, or require hospitalization may be considered a serious adverse drug experience when, based upon appropriate medical judgment, they may jeopardize the patient or subject and may require medical or surgical intervention.
Significant Communication	Any information that, in the opinion of the project team, may potentially affect the conduct of the study.
Site Assessment	Procedure to check that a trial site has the appropriate facilities, staff, and subject population to conduct a study in accordance with the Protocol and Good Clinical Practice. Also synonymous with Prestudy Assessment.
Site Close-out	Process of completing a clinical study at a trial site. Site close-out may start when the last subject has completed treatment/follow-up, but is not complete until all data queries relating to the site have been resolved.

Site Initiation	Procedures surrounding the start of a clinical study at a trial site (e.g., checking site facilities, delivery of clinical supplies, etc.). Unless waived by the client company, usually an initiation visit will be performed before any subjects are entered into a clinical study.
Site Visit Log	Document maintained at the trial site that records visits to the site by Sponsor representatives.
Source Data	All information in original records and certified copies of original records of clinical findings, observations, or other activities in a clinical trial necessary for the reconstruction and evaluation of the trial. Source data are contained in source documents (original records or certified copies).
Source Document	Original documents, data, and records (e.g., hospital records, clinical and office charts, laboratory notes, memoranda, subjects' diaries or evaluation checklists, pharmacy dispensing records, recorded data from automated instruments, copies or transcriptions certified after verification as being accurate and complete, microfiches, photographic negatives, microfilm or magnetic media, x-rays, subject files, and records kept at the pharmacy, at the laboratories, and at medico-technical departments involved in the clinical trial). (ICH)
Source Document Verification	Visual check of the data presented in a CRF against source documents to ensure that the source data exist and have been transcribed accurately.
Sponsor	An individual company, institution, or organization that takes responsibility for the initiation, management, and/or financing of a clinical trial. (ICH GCP 1.53)
Standard Operating Procedure (SOP)	An SOP is the detailed written instructions to achieve uniformity of the performance of a specific function. (ICH GCP 1.55)
Statistical Reviewer	Person who reviews the statistical aspects of the report. Should include product statistician and, as appropriate, Senior Biostatistician.
Study Coordinator	Person who generally handles the administrative responsibilities of a clinical trial at the site and acts as a liaison between the trial site and PPD.

Study Discontinuation   Premature closure of a trial site for operational reasons (e.g., poor recruitment, poor compliance), other reasons connected with the conduct of the study, or a change to the clinical development strategy.

Study Documentation   All documents supplied by an investigator or obtained by a client company that are required to ensure a site has been set up in accordance with Good Clinical Practice requirements.

Study Master File   Files containing documents and records (electronic or hard-copy) related to the general nature of the study, its development, and conduct.

Study Site Agreement   Documentation signed by the investigator or authorized person containing details of the work to be done, responsibilities of the investigator and client company, and general conduct of the study. Also synonymous with Statement of Agreement (SOA).

Study Supplies   Materials used in a study, including the investigational product(s).

Subinvestigator   Any individual member of the clinical trial team designated and supervised by the investigator at a trial site to perform critical trial-related procedures and/or to make important trial-related decisions (e.g., associates, residents, research fellows). (ICH)

Subject Identification List   Confidential list maintained by the trial site containing adequate information to uniquely identify a subject.

Subject/Trial Subject   An individual who participates in a clinical trial, either as a recipient of the investigational product(s) or as a control. (ICH)

Tape   The term tape is used to refer to magnetic tape but could refer to other backup media such as CD-ROM.

Trefoil   Radioactive warning sign

Trial Site   The location(s) where trial-related activities are actually conducted. (ICH)

Unexpected Adverse Event   Any AE that is not identified in nature, severity, or frequency in the current labeling or investigator's brochure, or that is not described in the risk information in the investigator's brochure, Protocol, or general study plan.

Universal Precautions Treating all human body fluids, specimens, and items contaminated with blood or body fluids as potentially infectious. Such material may contain bloodborne pathogens.

Validation The process of independently verifying the accuracy and completeness of the programming related to Biostatistics and Data Management deliverables.

Validation Program A program written to verify that a production program functions correctly.

Validator The Biostatistics team member(s) assigned to validate the Biostatistics and Data Management deliverables.

Visual Analog Scale A 100 mm line scale for indicating the level of pain being experienced by a patient, i.e., no pain to worst pain.

Whole Document Translation A whole document translation may be required for documents that will become a reference document at a study site. Examples are the translation of a Protocol, study subject diary cards, investigator's brochure, informed consent, etc.

Other Books of Interest

Pathways to Nursing

By Dennis C. Tucker and Paula Craig

This timely book provides a foundation in library and electronic research in the fields of nursing and allied health. It explains essential sources and techniques that can be used by nursing students, healthcare researchers, and nurse practitioners who need to gather information independently. *Pathways to Nursing* covers both physical libraries and online resources, showing how each can be used to its best advantage, and describes the six major components necessary to the development of information retrieval and utilization skills in this critical field.

Information Today, Inc. • 2004/266 pp/softbound • ISBN 1-57387-192-3 • $24.95

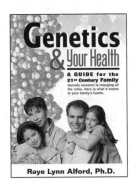

Genetics & Your Health: A Guide for the 21st Century Family

By Raye Lynn Alford, Ph.D., FACMG

Public interest in genetics has never been greater now that gene research promises to revolutionize medicine in the 21st century. In addition to the medical applications, the confidentiality of information and regulation of genetic technologies are hot-button topics. *Genetics and Your Health* will answer your questions about what the startling advances in genetic research, testing, and therapy really mean to today's family. Included is a directory to medical resources for genetics care, support, and information over the Internet, and the latest word on the Human Genome Project.

Medford Press/Plexus • 1999/266 pp/softbound • ISBN 0-9666748-1-2 • $19.95
Medford Press/Plexus • 1999/266 pp/hardbound • ISBN 0-9666748-2-0 • $29.95

Glossary of Terms Used in Informed Consent Documents for Pharmaceutical Trials: A Concise Reference for Clinical Researchers

By Deborrah Norris

This invaluable reference provides more than 1500 medical terms and their lay language definitions. The book also includes a detailed, thoroughly researched history and analysis of the informed consent document, as well as explicit instructions on how to compose such a document.

"The important contribution of this book is that it will facilitate translation of technical terms to more generally accessible language. In this way, it will assist clinicians, investigators, members of institutional review boards, and others in their efforts to improve the process of informed consent."

—Robert J. Levine, MD
Author, *Ethics and Regulation of Clinical Research*

Plexus Publishing, Inc. • 1996/70 pp/softbound • 0-9631310-3-6 • $39.95

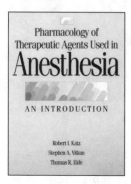

Pharmacology of Therapeutic Agents Used in Anesthesia: An Introduction

By Robert I. Katz, Stephen A. Vitkun, and Thomas R. Eide

Here is a practical guide to all classes of therapeutic agents the anesthesiologist may encounter or administer during the perioperative period. This concise reference elucidates the pharmacology of each class of drugs and provides the anesthesiologist with the basic footing needed to understand the clinical implications of administering non-anesthetic agents in conjunction with anesthesia. This substantive yet accessible text is one from which both practicing anesthesiologists and residents can learn—and relearn—important principles of pharmacology in patient care.

"An eminently readable guide to the applied pharmacology of anesthesia. I highly recommend it."

—Albert J. Saubermann, MD
Professor and Chairman/Department of Anesthesiology
Albert Einstein College of Medicine of Yeshiva University
Montefiore Medical Center

Plexus Publishing, Inc. • 1994/311 pp/hardbound • 0-9631310-2-8 • $68.00

A Dictionary of Natural Products

By George Macdonald Hocking, Ph.D.

A Dictionary of Natural Products is primarily devoted to an arrangement and explanation of terms relating to natural, non-artificial crude drugs from the vegetable, animal, and mineral kingdoms. This volume presents over 18,000 entries of medicinal, pharmaceutical, and related products appearing on the market as raw materials or occurring in drug stores, folk medical practice, and in chemical manufacturing processes.

Plexus Publishing, Inc. • 1997/1,024 pp/hardbound • ISBN 0-937548-31-6 • $139.50
(A $6 shipping and handling fee will be added to the cost.)

Biology Digest

Biology Digest is a comprehensive abstracts journal covering all the life sciences. Each monthly issue contains over 300 abstracts which are, in essence, individual digests of articles and research reports gathered from worldwide sources. Important information is retained in the abstracts to give a precise, inclusive summary of the original material.

Biology Digest was specially created to meet the needs of high school and undergraduate college students. It provides easy access to new scientific developments at a comprehension level appropriate for students. However, *Biology Digest* has proved to be useful to biologists at all levels—professional and amateur alike.

Biology Digest and its companion databases are available electronically through a special arrangement with NewsBank, Inc. For more information on the ScienceSource Collection, contact NewsBank, Inc., at (800) 762-8182, or e-mail sales@newsbank.com.

Plexus Publishing, Inc. • Volume 31 (2004/05) • Monthly (September-May) • ISSN 0095-2958
1 year $149.00
(New subscribers qualify for the special introductory price of $119.00 or may purchase volumes 30 & 31 as the "Get Started Package" for $199.00.)

For a publications catalog,
call 609-654-6500, or
log onto www.plexuspublishing.com

NOTES

NOTES

NOTES